Deliberate Soccer Practice

50 Defending Football Exercises to Improve Decision-Making

Ray Power

BENNION
KEARNY

Published by Bennion Kearny Limited
6 Woodside
Churnet View Road
Oakamoor
ST10 3AE

www.BennionKearny.com

Deliberate Practice & Defending

In the first book of this series, *Deliberate Soccer Practice: 50 Passing and Possession Exercises to Improve Decision Making*, we explored the need for your soccer sessions to allow your players the opportunity to practice *deliberately*.

Deliberate, or purposeful, practice goes way beyond what we may normally see from 'soccer' sessions – lapping pitches, long queues, waiting your turn and the inevitable insistence that players "follow their pass". Deliberate practice is about the game – the real game – and how to absorb players in decision-making whilst ensuring they are physically and mentally engaged and challenged – *for every single moment*!

This book, alongside the other books in the series, is not theoretical, but the theories that underpin the training methods here have been studied, practiced and implemented within youth and adult soccer, and work to accelerate learning. They make players, and their improvement, the centerpiece of the training program; not the coach and his ego or instruction.

We noted in the previous book the need to maximise *returns*, make practices realistic and to give players challenges and problems to solve. These factors work together to accelerate player development by keeping all players physically involved, and critically, *cognitively engaged*. As a fraternity, soccer coaches are good at working players physically, 'drilling' them, but often unknowingly neglect the development of thinkers and decision-makers. By focusing on returns, we quickly move away from situations where we organise our sessions with queues and "waiting your turn" to ones that encourage players to solve problems while replicating the game and all its many, many variables.

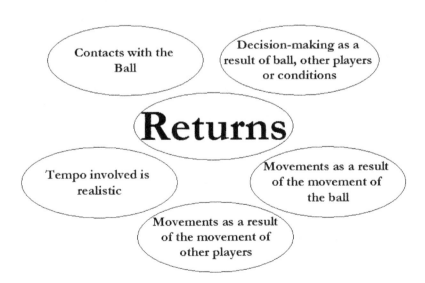

Defending

First of all, although this book is about defending, it is not only for 'defenders'. Just like the upcoming edition on attacking is not solely for forward players. Both defending and attacking are key components for the whole team. Just watch forward Luis Suarez when his team are out of possession, or defender Sergio Ramos when in possession. All players, goalkeepers included, need to have the ability to attack and defend, although precise positional requirements and foci will, of course, differ.

Defending Principles of Play

Regardless of what formation you play, what system or tactics you employ, or what your attacking or defensive strategy is, the game is dictated by the *principles of play*. These principles are what govern the game. So whether you prefer to attack centrally or use the wide areas to get crosses in, or whether you like your team to defend deep or to *gegenpress*, soccer remains underpinned by these principles.

Throughout this book, although your defending philosophy may be challenged or you wish to defend a different way, we will constantly refer back to these principles. Broadly, we speak about defending either being organized or disorganized. When organized, our team shape is in place and the team can defend as per an identified strategy. When disorganized however, we need to defend differently and make different decisions that allow teammates to recover and which offer time for the team to reorganize. Defending when organized is a more comfortable place to be, but having to defend when disorganized is inevitable.

Defending is often neglected both within local grassroots soccer and even in elite academy environments, largely due to some miscomprehension of the topic. Some coaches tell me that players find defending "boring", while even established player development coaches will feel the necessity to focus purely on technique with the ball – passing, dribbling, crossing, shooting, etc. What we must understand, however, is that practices that can be used while coaching defending are no different than those used when coaching any other topic. After all, if some players are focusing on defending, then the others are naturally attacking.

Practices in this Book

Along with the returns above, I have outlined four further rules for the 50 practices within this book. Each aspect is essential in making the practices both *realistic and deliberate*:

1. Transitions MUST be Included

Although there is an obvious focus on the defending aspect of the game here, coaches must be careful not to treat defending as an isolated part of the game. Defending is one of the games' *Four Phases*, which includes attacking and two transition phases. Transitions occur the *moment* a team either loses the ball or regains the ball.

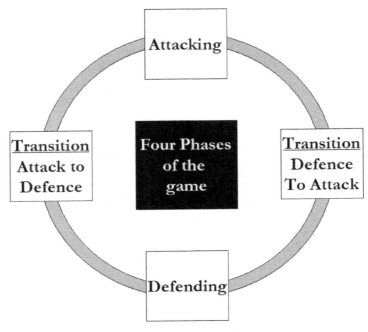

The Four Phases of the Game

Attacking, Defending, Transition to Attack, Transition to Defend

Including attacking and transitions in your defending sessions is absolutely critical. A practice exercise should not grind to a halt when a defender wins possession, or when he simply whacks it away or out of play. He must be able to transition and must have the possibility of counter-attacking. If the possibility of transitioning is not present, then the game realism of what you are doing is seriously flawed. *Players will defend differently depending on what happens when they regain possession.*

By simply devising exercises where all players involved are both attacking and defending, there will naturally be moments of transition. These moments occur organically in any game and are an integral part of matches. The importance of these transitions is growing more and more within the elite soccer environment. Learning to attack while a team is disorganized, and conversely being able to defend effectively while you reorganize having lost possession, prove to be some of the most critical moments within soccer matches.

Allowing the defending players to attack means that they will push out, disorganizing themselves in the process, and will then need to react realistically to losing the ball by making recovery runs, delaying attacks, and defending when outnumbered – all intrinsically vital parts to learning and practicing realistic defending. This creates a game environment where there is a natural ebb and flow, there is a competitive edge, where technique is, in turn, an explicit outcome. Further to the objectives we set out above, all 50 exercises in this book will contain natural transitions.

Managed properly, like any training exercise or game, players will not be bored and you can also give them lots and lots of practice with the ball at their feet.

2. Opposed

Unlike the attacking topics we deliver, like passing or dribbling, where we may include unopposed practices, teaching defending without opposition is difficult and offers very little in terms of *returns*. Sure, we can talk about body shape, positioning, covering players, etc, but this has got to be in reference to the ball, the opponent with the ball, the position of his (and your) teammates, and the position on the pitch. How you defend 1v1 is very different when in the opposition half, compared to when it is in your own penalty box for example! Defending needs context, and that context is the ball, the opposition, and your fellow defenders.

I once witnessed a very well-intentioned coach set up a practice where he put a back four in place to defend a full-size goal against six attackers. In principle, I have no issue with this, in fact I love that he outnumbered the defenders to put them under real stress, but critically, he did not include a goalkeeper! The challenge for the players then is instantly flawed. They cannot operate as an organized back four without a goalkeeper in position. The opposition do not need to break down the defence as they could simply play the ball over or through them for a simple goal. In addition, it changes the offside rule, and the chance of the goalkeeper helping you defend successfully by catching a cross, running out to gather a through pass, or simply giving information to his defenders.

All this feeds into a single aim of this book – to allow players to practice and improve in the closest way we can to the real game. The problems they will be challenged to solve will occur in the 100-mile-per-hour action of the real game – and all the problems and variables that match action throws up. We may not always include a goalkeeper as certain practices are structured differently, but the element of realism versus returns will not be compromised.

Importantly also, the defenders or defending team in this book will never overload the opposition. We will however constantly overload the defenders – i.e. have more players attacking than defending. This 'stress' for defenders allows them to practice being compact, prioritize who to mark, judge when to mark space or when to tightly mark players, and when to pressure the ball to thwart a goal-scoring opportunity. Even in the 1 v 1 practices we will look at, we will constantly look for ways to cause further 'interference' within the session. The more chaotic the problem-solving environment, the better a player will become.

3. Competitive

The idea of competition, in youth soccer in particular, is hotly debated everywhere – does winning matter? If we only focus on winning, do we end up fast-tracking the big kids rather than technical ones?

I discussed this very issue in chapter one of *Making the Ball Roll – A Complete Guide to Youth Football for the Aspiring Soccer Coach*. It was the first chapter for a reason due to its important position in the development of young players. It is vital that coaches fully understand the difference between harnessing the naturally highly competitive nature of kids, and using winning on a game-day as a measure of the players or the coach himself. In a very good article, Nick Levett (now Talent ID Manager at the English FA) speaks about "Child-Centred Competition" as opposed to winning at all costs.

So, if kids are naturally competitive – use this in your soccer sessions. Use this natural enthusiasm to keep the tempo high, the challenge real, and the motivation of the players elevated. Keep a score whenever possible. You can count goals, challenge one team to beat the opponent's score, set a time limit, play the best out of three, etc. By adding a score, it makes the practice matter, but without making losing the end of the world. If the practice matters to the players, it automatically starts to reflect the pressure of a game environment, without the pressure of the coach needing to win, or a league table to worry about. This then further adds to the realism, variability, and tempo of the session. Along with keeping score, you may measure *time* (you are 1-0 up in a final with five minutes left – can you keep a clean sheet and hang on to win the game?), or *attempts* (the attackers will have five attempts to score – how many attacks can you thwart?).

The 50 exercises herein will include these competitive edges.

4. Include 'Critical' Moments

In my roles as coach, coach mentor, and coach educator, I see a lot of sessions. This experience is wonderful as it forces me to analyse what works, what does not, and what – if anything – needs to be thrown away.

When coaching defending, I observe lots of organized exercises, but rarely ones where defending becomes *critical*. By critical I mean the point where a defender *has* to make a block, challenge, tackle, interception, etc. or a goal *will* be conceded. By ensuring the other three points are in place (transitions, opposed, and competitive) we create situations where it is a 'do or die' moment for the players – where it is *critical* that they foil the attack. No player should be allowed to willingly accept a goal being scored against them, even in a training session.

Throughout this book, we will challenge the players to keep the ball out of the net in these critical do-or-die situations. In real game situations, the vast majority of goals are scored from within the central area in front of goal. Almost 80% of all these goals come from either one or two-touch finishes. Below is a graph from the 2014 World Cup that I used in *Soccer Tactics 2014 – What the World Cup Taught Us*. Although taken from one competition of only 64 games, this reflects the nature of where goals are scored from throughout competitions from youth to the professional game. So, with a huge percentage of goals coming from a particular area, and generally being one or two-touch finishes, we need to put defenders in situations where they are constantly dealing with this threat. The ability to mark, track movements, block, tackle, cover the goal line or maybe even throw your body in front of a goal-bound shot needs practicing.

Where World Cup 2014 Goals Came From

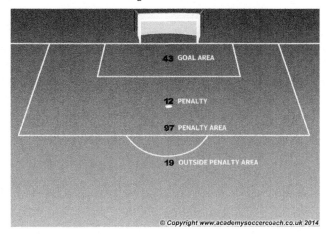

The illustration above features the areas where goals were scored from during the 2014 World Cup. What are the implications for coaches working on defending?

Conclusion

The following 50 practices will develop from 1 v 1 defending practices, right up to team practices, small-sided games, tactical phases of play and 'scenario' training. All these sessions put an emphasis on defending *deliberately* – we make these sessions difficult for players, but in a way that challenges them, engages them and makes them work. Enjoy the sessions – now who said defending was boring!?

Key

- - - - ->	Pass / Shoot
→	Off the ball movement
⤵	Curled Pass
⤴	Lofted Pass

Individual Defending Exercises

Section one begins with individual defending, mainly in 1 v 1 situations, but also when outnumbered.

It is very important that players, regardless of their position, can defend in 1 v 1 situations for a variety of reasons. Not only are there lots of frequent 1 v 1 occurrences within games, the ability and decisions made by the first defender will impact upon the defending of the whole group, and generally should set the tone for the reaction and set up of the whole team. If he presses the ball, for example, it can prompt the rest of the team to press and condense the play. If he shows the opponent inside, the rest of the team can defend more narrowly, mark tighter, and ensure there are enough bodies centrally to contest possession and regain the ball.

1: One v One Competition

PURPOSE OF SESSION:

To help players defend in 1v1 situations. The constant rotation of players and opposition means players get a variety of challenges technically, physically, tactically and mentally. This is also excellent for the social development of your group

INITIAL SET-UP:

- Divide your group into pairs.

- There should be a channel for each pair to play 1v1 in.

- If a player wins, he moves right, if he loses he moves left. If the game ends in a draw, players play a quick game of rock-paper-scissors (social corner).

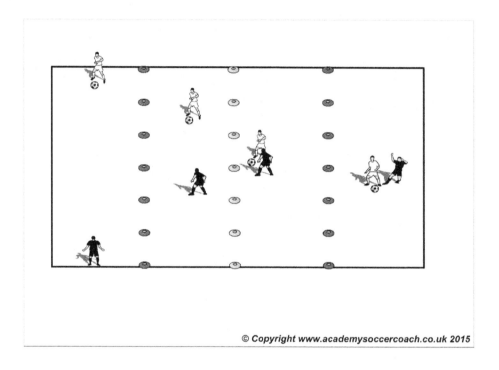

INSTRUCTIONS:

- Black starts with the ball and passes to White.

- White attempts to dribble past Black and score by reaching the end line.

- **TRANSITION:** Once Black wins the ball back, he can score by dribbling to the opposite end line. Thus, there is a constant change between who defends and who attacks.

- Each game should last 45 – 60 seconds.

PROGRESSIONS:

1. Natural progressions occur as you are constantly changing opponents. This can be very tiring so natural breaks as players change opponents and channels should be used.

2. The coach can remove the cones and play 1 v 1, but with further interference from another pair. Or, of course, you can progress it to a 2 v 2 competition.

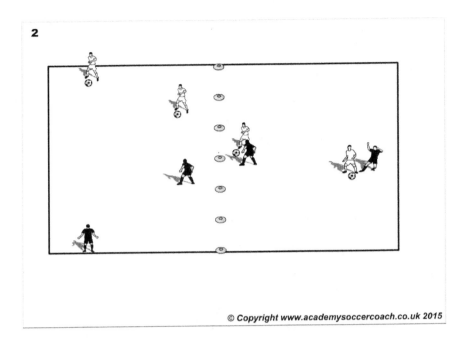

CHALLENGES / QUESTIONS FOR PLAYERS:

- Can you force or 'deflect' the attacker in the direction you want him to go (surfer position)?

- If the attacker is close to the sidelines, can you force him out?

- If the attacker is close to the scoring line, or goes past you, can you 'critically' defend?

- Unless critically defending, keep the ball in play and look to counter-attack quickly once you have regained it.

- Once you have scored, can you transition quickly to stop your opponent countering the counter-attack?

SCORING:

Each player gets a point for stopping the ball on the end line.

CAUTION:

This game can become highly competitive! Watch out for bickering and cheating! The game is also excellent for social development and resolving disputes!

2: One v One Defending the Zone

PURPOSE OF SESSION:

For players to practice defending in 1 v 1 situations with greater *interference* than session 1.

INITIAL SET-UP:

- Set up an area split into three zones.
- Half the group is in White and half in Black.
- Players play 1 v 1 all over the area.

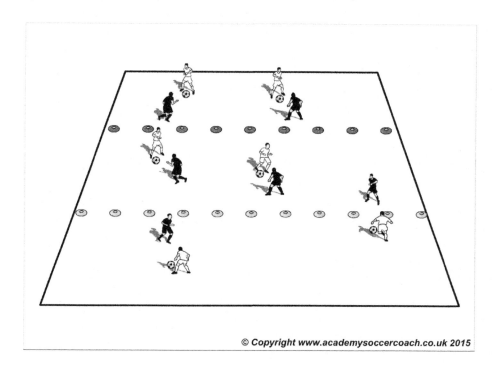

INSTRUCTIONS:

- Whites start with a ball and attempt to dribble past their teammate into the next zone.
- **TRANSITION:** If defender regains possession, he can dribble the ball back over the end line. Players must not be allowed to just kick the ball out of the area (encouraged to transition and counter-attack).
- Change the players playing against each other on a regular basis.

PROGRESSIONS:

1. Defenders and attackers work as pairs. Either defender can tackle / defend against either attacker, allowing players to work in tandem.

2. Remove coned areas and attack / defend the end lines.

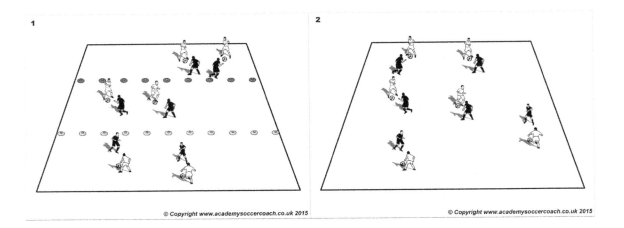

© Copyright www.academysoccercoach.co.uk 2015

© Copyright www.academysoccercoach.co.uk 2015

CHALLENGES / QUESTIONS FOR PLAYERS:

- Can you dictate what the attacker does by deflecting him into an area where *you* want him to go?

- Can you force the attacker out of play if he is close to the sidelines?

- Can you critically defend when the attacker is in a dangerous position and close to scoring a goal?

- If the attacker goes past you, can you recover to stop him scoring again?

- When defending as a pair, or in a group, can you communicate effectively and prioritise when to pass players on?

- When you regain possession, can you counter-attack quickly, rather than just putting the ball out of play?

SCORING:

The attacker gets one point for every zone he progresses through. The defender gets a point for regaining possession and successfully counter-attacking. Offer two points for successful counter-attacks if necessary to encourage transition.

CAUTION:

One v one exercises can be more tiring than you think. Use regular drinks breaks and change the pairs intermittently to freshen the game up and allow players a short rest.

3: One v One Prevent Turning

PURPOSE OF SESSION:

Players practice the art of marking, preventing their opponent turning, but also perfect when to screen a forward pass, and when to mark tightly.

INITIAL SET-UP:

- Players essentially work in small groups of four (two outside greys plus one Black defender and one White attacker on the inside).

- One of the greys has a ball.

- Defenders mark 1 v 1 in the central area.

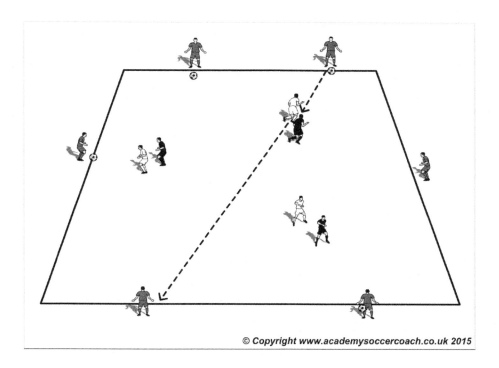

INSTRUCTIONS:

- Outside grey starts with the ball and looks to feed it to the White attacker.

- The White attacker attempts to get the ball to a free grey on the other side of the square.

- The defender aims to stop his opponent turning and scoring.

- **TRANSITION:** When the defender regains possession, he passes to a free grey.

- Change attackers, defenders and outside players periodically.

PROGRESSIONS:

1. White attackers can 'lend' the ball to a free grey. Defender must track the movement of

the attacker to a) stop him receiving the ball back, or b) stop him scoring.

2. Greys can now pass from side to side to score. Defenders must position themselves to screen / intercept this pass, as it is a priority, rather than tight marking. Once the pass goes to the White, he can then press and complete the previous two challenges.

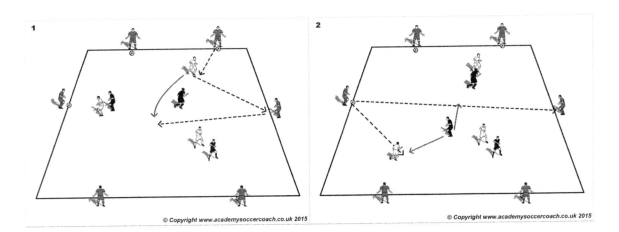

CHALLENGES / QUESTIONS FOR PLAYERS:

- Can you stop the attacker turning?

- Can you decide when to mark him tightly or when to mark him loosely and *travel as the ball travels*?

- Can you see both the attacker *and* the ball *most* of the time?

- Can you track (either physically or mentally) the movements of the attacker?

- Can you prioritize when to screen and intercept passes, and when to tightly mark the attacker?

- When *critically* defending, can you tackle, block, slide or disturb the ball or attacker?

- When you regain possession, be clinical by finding a free grey with your pass.

SCORING:

Attackers score by getting the ball from one grey to the opposite one. Defenders counter-attack by winning the ball and finding a free grey to pass to.

CAUTION:

Change players' roles intermittently, though your may prioritize certain positions for certain roles. For example, you may want a midfielder defending centrally to help him practice his decisions around whether to screen forward passes or whether to mark tightly.

4: One v One Recovery

PURPOSE OF SESSION:

Learning to defend 1 v 1, with a clear focus on defenders recovering to goal to defend *critically*.

INITIAL SET-UP:

- Two players, one attacker and one defender on the edge of the penalty box.
- A coach or a third player starts between them with a ball.
- A goalkeeper defends a big goal. Two smaller goals are placed just outside the box.

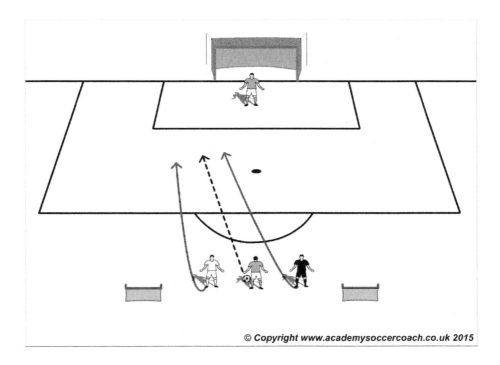

© Copyright www.academysoccercoach.co.uk 2015

INSTRUCTIONS:

- The coach feeds a ball towards the goal, varying the weight and angle each time.
- The attacker and defender race to compete for the ball – having initially faced the opposite direction.
- **TRANSITION:** If the defender gets to the ball first, or wins possession back, he can attack and score in either of the smaller goals.

PROGRESSIONS:

1. The coach feeds the ball, though this time in the air.
2. If there is no goalkeeper available, can the attacker dribble through any of the yellow

gates? Can the defender look to force his opponent away from goal?

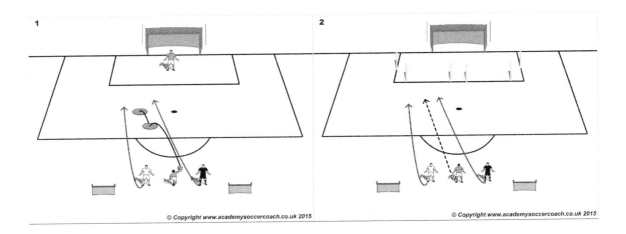

CHALLENGES / QUESTIONS FOR PLAYERS:

- Can the defender win the race and get to the ball first?

- If not, can he defend the goal, deflecting the attacker away from goal?

- If the defender wins the ball, can he counter-attack and score in one of the small goals?

- When the ball is fed aerially, can the defender use this to his advantage?

- Can the defender decide whether to recover straight to the ball, or straight to a position between the ball and goal? In particular, can he make this decision when faced with opponents who may be quicker / slower?

- If the attacker loses possession, can he recover to stop the defender counter-attacking?

SCORING:

The attacker scores past the goalkeeper in the full-size goals, or dribbles through the gates. The defender scores in either of the two small goals. If one player is dominant in terms of the score line, change the value of a goal (for example, the attacker will score three points for a goal past the goalkeeper).

CAUTION:

Rotate players to allow them time to rest after successive sprints.

5: One v One Continuous

PURPOSE OF SESSION:

Players defend 1 v 1 in variable circumstances, against various opponents.

INITIAL SET-UP:

- The group is split in half – half defenders and half attackers.

- Numerous footballs are placed in a central area in the middle of the grid.

- A goal is set up on the borders for each defender to protect.

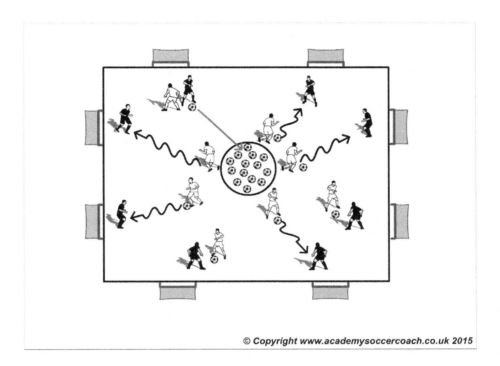

INSTRUCTIONS:

- Whites collect a ball from the central area and attack a defender 1 v 1. The Black defenders look to defend their assigned goal.

- **TRANSITION:** If defender wins possession, can he drive with the ball and deposit it back in the area? He is then required to recover quickly to defend his own goal again.

PROGRESSIONS:

1. Rotate attackers clockwise / anti-clockwise to face different defenders.
2. Any attacker can attack and play against any defender he chooses.

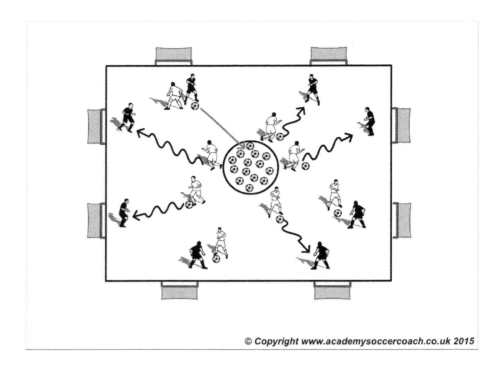

CHALLENGES / QUESTIONS FOR PLAYERS:

- Using the 'surfer' body position, can you force the attacker in the direction you want him to go, maybe onto his least preferred foot?

- Can you force the attacker away from your goal, either further across the grid, or out of play?

- If the attacker is close to the goal, can you 'critically' defend?

- When any attacker can attack you, can you constantly be aware of the most critical danger to your goal?

- Unless critically defending, keep the ball in play and look to counter-attack quickly once you have regained it.

- Can your first touch be positive to counter-attack quickly?

SCORING:

The attacker gets a point for every goal he scores, the defender for every ball he intercepts and deposits back into the central zone.

CAUTION:

This exercise can be quite frantic. Observe one defender at a time to give you clarity about their performance. If you try to observe the whole group, you can end up missing more than you see.

6: One v One Marking in Box

PURPOSE OF SESSION:

To allow players to practice marking their opponent, specifically in the penalty area.

INITIAL SET-UP:

- Four servers at each corner of the penalty area. Goalkeeper defends the goal.

- One White defender versus one Black attacker in the penalty area.

- Three smaller goals are set up outside the penalty area.

© Copyright www.academysoccercoach.co.uk 2015

INSTRUCTIONS:

- Servers take it in turns to pass the ball into the attacker who attempts to score, preferably with one or two touches. The defender must mark, intercept and defend as necessary.

- **TRANSITION:** If the defender wins the ball back, he can attack and score in any of the three smaller goals. All attackers can recover to stop him doing so.

- Change the player combinations regularly.

PROGRESSIONS:

1. Servers pass the ball amongst themselves before playing into the striker, changing the position of the defender in the process. If it is possible, the defender can intercept any of these passes.

2. The attackers are now challenged to play a pass in the air to offer both the attacker and defender a different challenge.

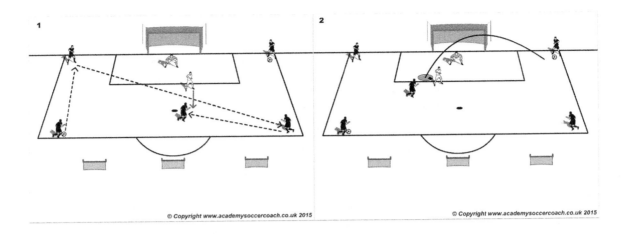

CHALLENGES / QUESTIONS FOR PLAYERS:

- When do you mark touch tight?

- When do you allow space between you and the attacker to prioritize defending the goal?

- If you are not touch tight, can you 'travel as the ball travels' – i.e. be able to make up the ground between you and the attacker as the ball is delivered?

- Can you alter your defensive position in relation to the server, the ball, the attacker and the danger?

- Can you *critically* defend to stop the striker scoring if he receives possession?

- If you intercept, can you counter-attack and score before the attacking team recovers?

SCORING:

The attacker gets one point for every goal he scores. The defender gets a point for scoring a counter-attacking goal.

CAUTION:

Do not allow the defender to just follow the striker touch-tight around the penalty area! Not only is this poor defending, as the striker will get away from him, players that do this tend to just foul the attacker in this training exercise.

7: One v One Chaos

PURPOSE OF SESSION:

To help players defend in 1 v 1 situations in constantly changing, 'chaotic' conditions.

INITIAL SET-UP:

- Divide your group into pairs.
- Players defend an end line and attack the opposite one.

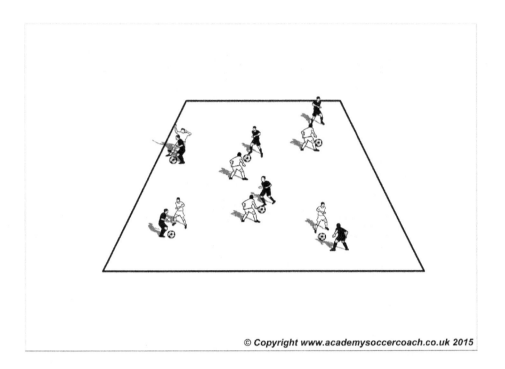

INSTRUCTIONS:

- Players are paired and play 1 v 1 in the defined area.
- Any player can move anywhere within the grid, meaning players will have to defend with lots of traffic around them.
- Players score by dribbling the ball to the opposite end line.
- **TRANSITION:** Once the defender wins the ball back, he immediately attacks his opponent's end line, and then recovers back to a defensive position.

PROGRESSIONS:

1. Change the partners working against each other. This poses defenders with different problems on each occasion.
2. This practice can easily be progressed to be played in a 2 v 2 format.

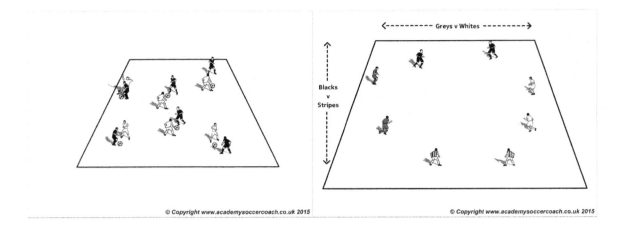

CHALLENGES / QUESTIONS FOR PLAYERS:

- Can you deal with defending 1 v 1, but with other players 'interfering'?

- Can you show or deflect the attacker in the direction you want him to go (surfer position)?

- Can you force the attacker out of play if he is in possession near the sidelines?

- If the attacker is close to the scoring line, or goes past you, can you *critically* defend?

- Unless critically defending, keep the ball in play and look to counter-attack quickly once you have regained it.

- Once you have scored, can you transition quickly to stop your opponent countering the counter-attack?

SCORING:

Each player gets a point for stopping the ball on their opponent's end line.

CAUTION:

Challenge players to deal with the traffic, interference and randomness of other players affecting the way they defend.

8: Critical One v One

PURPOSE OF SESSION:

For defenders to be constantly aware of 1 v 1 threats around them.

INITIAL SET-UP:

- Playing area with eight orange gates placed randomly throughout the inside, each defended by one White player (alter numbers to suit).

- All Black attackers have a ball each.

- Blue-gated goals are also set up around the perimeter of the area

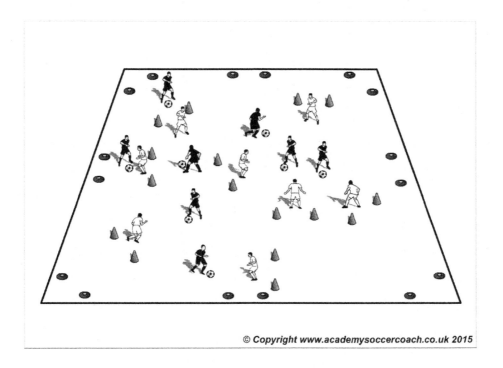

© Copyright www.academysoccercoach.co.uk 2015

INSTRUCTIONS:

- Each White defender defends one of the internal orange, gated goals as they play 1 v 1 against a Black attacker.

- Defenders must stop the attackers dribbling through the gate. Attackers can attempt to dribble through any orange gate.

- **TRANSITION:** If the Whites regain possession, they can break out and counter-attack through any of the blue gates around the perimeter. Blacks must track the run and look to regain the ball if possible, and start another quick attack.

PROGRESSIONS:

1. Reduce the number of orange gates and number of defenders, thus increasing the number of attackers.

2. Reintroduce the omitted gates, but keep the defenders outnumbered. Defenders must now defend all gates.

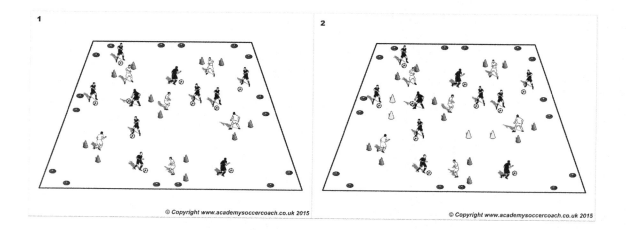

© Copyright www.academysoccercoach.co.uk 2015   © Copyright www.academysoccercoach.co.uk 2015

CHALLENGES / QUESTIONS FOR PLAYERS:

- Can you defend you own gate and deflect or force the attacker away from goal?

- Can you be aware of a threat to your goal both in front of you and behind you (open body)?

- Can you defend in front of your gate, rather than on the goal line? This will stop an attacker powering over the line, and give you some space to recover if necessary.

- When outnumbered, can you prioritize the greatest threat to your goal?

- Can you work together with other defenders when outnumbered – sharing responsibility for the spare goals?

- If you win possession back, can you counter attack quickly and run the ball through a blue outside gate? When you have done this, can you recover quickly into a defensive position?

SCORING:

Attackers score by dribbling the ball through the internal orange-gated goals. Defenders score by counter-attacking and running with the ball through the outer blue gates.

CAUTION:

This practice can get very chaotic and present a great cognitive challenge for the players. Encourage defenders to be strong-minded and to concern themselves with defending their goal and counter-attacking as appropriate.

9: Defending when Outnumbered 1 v 2

PURPOSE OF SESSION:

Players are introduced to Defending when Outnumbered principles.

INITIAL SET-UP:

- Design an area with two goals (must be goals to attack and defend, not end lines).
- Two attackers v one defender.
- (Shaded lines are for visual purposes only).

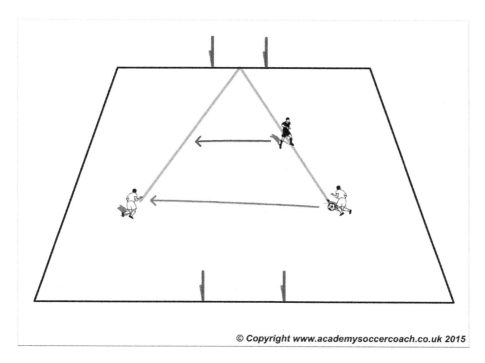

INSTRUCTIONS:

- White attackers start with the ball and try to score against the lone Black defender.
- To protect the goal, the Black defender tries to block a direct path between the ball and goal, and will stay within the imaginary inverted grey lines (unless he can leave to regain possession or isolate an opponent 1 v 1).
- **TRANSITION:** Once the defender regains possession he can score in the opponent's goal. It will be very difficult for him to start an attack alone and score, but give the players a challenge!

PROGRESSIONS:

1. Add regions in the wide areas where the defender can force or dictate the attacker into (he scores a point if he can force the attacker there).
2. The defender can dribble through the gates to score, putting an emphasis on him needing

to recover quickly into a defensive position.

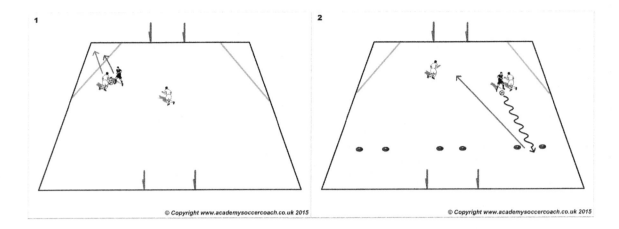

CHALLENGES / QUESTIONS FOR PLAYERS:

- Can you be patient and *delay* the attacks of the opposition?

- Can you *deny* the attackers from scoring directly by manoeuvring into positions between the ball and goal?

- Can you get close enough to one player to dictate or force him away from goal?

- Can you use any opportunity to defend strongly and win the ball?

- Can you counter-attack quickly and sensibly (considering you are outnumbered and will need to recover quickly) and score a goal?

SCORING:

Attackers get a point for scoring a goal, the defender gets two points for a goal and a further point for forcing an attacker into the wide regions or off the pitch.

CAUTION:

Rotate the roles of the players frequently so it is not the same player constantly outnumbered, while giving them enough ongoing practice of the challenge.

10: Mixed Defending

PURPOSE OF SESSION:

A 'carrousel' session to challenge players in a variety of defending situations.

INITIAL SET-UP:

- Divide an outer area into four segments.

- Two small goals for the defender to defend in the bottom; outnumbered practices.

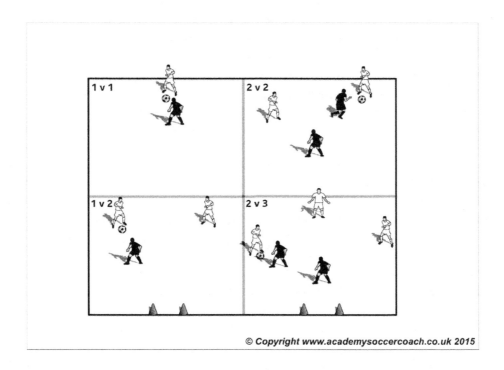

© Copyright www.academysoccercoach.co.uk 2015

INSTRUCTIONS:

- Players play 1 v 1, 2 v 2, 1 v 2 and 2 v 3 in different segments.

- Attackers attempt to score by dribbling to the line (top games with even attackers and defenders) or by scoring in the small goals (outnumbered, bottom games).

- **TRANSITION:** When defenders win the ball back, they run the ball to the end line to score.

PROGRESSIONS:

1. Rotate players around the grids to allow them to experience all challenges.

2. Prioritise players in certain grids – for example, full-backs play 1 v 1, center-backs 2 v 2, midfielders 2 v 3 and strikers 1 v 2.

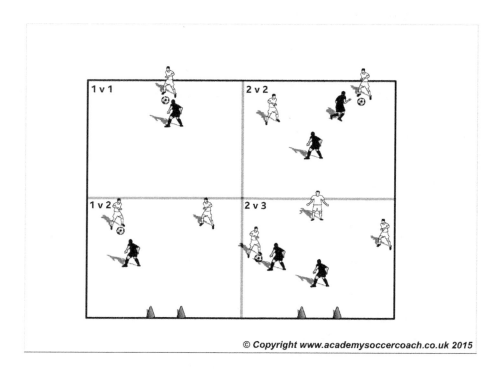

CHALLENGES / QUESTIONS FOR PLAYERS:

- Can you adapt to the constantly changing defending conditions?
- Can players display an understanding of the Defending, and Defending when Outnumbered, Principles of Play
- Challenges from other related practices in this book can also be used.

SCORING:

Attackers get a point for stopping the ball on the end line / scoring through small goals. Defenders score by counter-attacking and stopping the ball on the opposite end line.

CAUTION:

Adapt the set-up, number of games, or the games used to ensure that all your players are involved all of the time.

Small Group Defending

With players now comfortable when defending in 1 v 1 situations, we can now increase the challenge to defending in small groups. The principles of 1 v 1 defending will remain present, but there will be further challenges and principles with extra attackers and defenders in the games.

Like the previous section, we will look at defending with equal numbers, but also defending when outnumbered. We will increase our focus on how to defend when disorganized and transitioning as a group between attack and defence, and also transitioning between defence and attack.

11: Two v Two

PURPOSE OF SESSION:

Players can practice basic defending as a pair and the principles of press / delay and cover.

INITIAL SET-UP:

- Two Blacks v two Whites in the playing area.
- Each pair attacks and defends a goal with a gate either side of the goal.

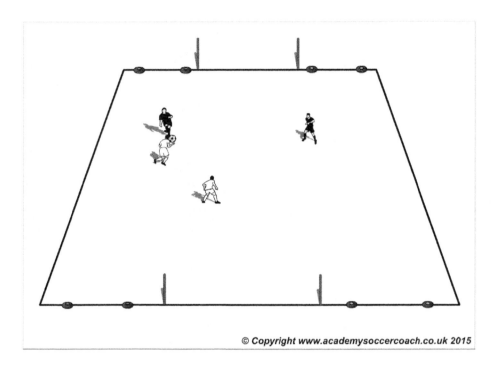

© Copyright www.academysoccercoach.co.uk 2015

INSTRUCTIONS:

- Play 2 v 2 using the goals only to begin with.
- As one defender presses, the second takes up a covering position to protect the goal / forward pass. He must be able to 'travel as the ball travels' and press the other opponent.
- **TRANSITION:** If the defenders win the ball back they look to counter-attack and score. The opposition pair then become the defenders and defend in the same manner.

PROGRESSIONS:

1. Introduce the opportunity to score by dribbling through side gates, as well as scoring in the main goal. This increases the options for attackers (pass, shoot, dribble, run with the ball) allowing more challenges for defenders. The first defender may force the attacker inside to encourage an interception of a forward pass or shot, or he may force the

attacker outside to win the ball in a 1 v 1 or to force the attacker out of play.

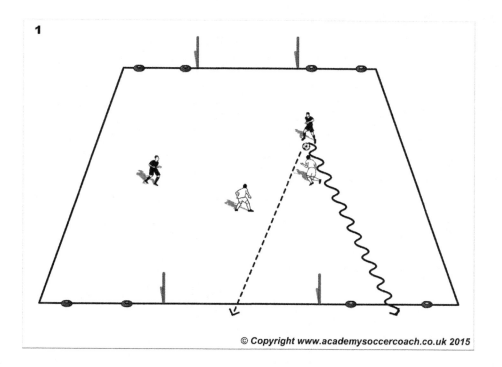

CHALLENGES / QUESTIONS FOR PLAYERS:

- Can you show the principles of the first defender pressing and second defender taking up a cover position?

- Can you encourage the opposition to play passes sideways?

- Can you encourage forward passes where you can intercept the ball, or dribbles where you can win possession 1 v 1?

- Can the second defender communicate effectively with the first ("force him wide", "force him inside", "must win" etc.)?

- When you become disorganized, can you recover to protect the goal?

- If you intercept, can you counter-attack and score before the attacking team recovers?

SCORING:

Count goals scored in goals and points scored by dribbling through gates. Players get points by either scoring through the main goal, or by dribbling through the outside gates (when relevant).

CAUTION:

Ensure both teams defend correctly. The attacking team should recover and defend with the same intent as the team that has just defended.

12: Two v Two Stay on Your Feet

PURPOSE OF SESSION:

A 2 v 2 exercise designed to promote players staying on their feet, rather than going to ground.

INITIAL SET-UP:

- Set up the playing area with each pair defending two small goals.

- Include an end zone in front of the goals.

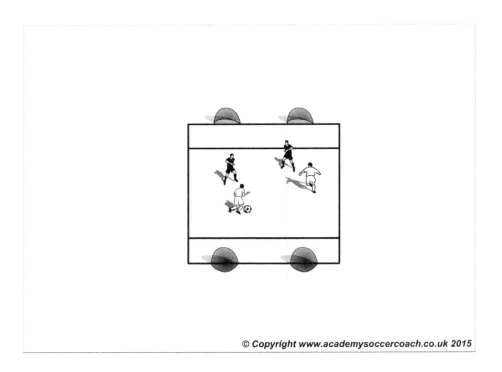

INSTRUCTIONS:

- Players play 2 v 2 and look to score in either small goal.

- Players should mark, track forward runs, etc, but should not go to ground in the playing area.

- Players can only go to ground when *critically* defending in the end zone area in front of goal.

- **TRANSITION:** If the defending pair win the ball back, they can counter-attack and score. The opposition must recover and defend their goals.

PROGRESSIONS:

1. Adapt to use exercise 11, with no restrictions and observe whether players can position themselves better and stay on their feet more frequently.

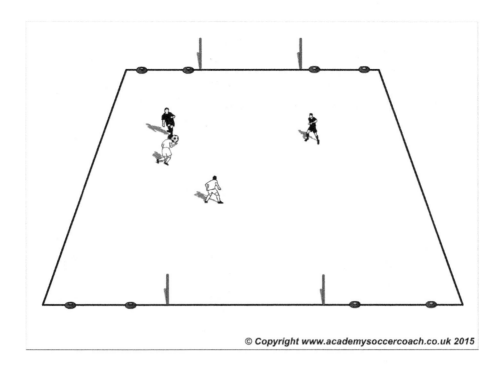

CHALLENGES / QUESTIONS FOR PLAYERS:

- Use Defending Principles of Play and challenges from exercise 11.

- Can you stay on your feet unless you have to go to ground when *critically* defending?

SCORING:

Count goals scored, or goals and dribbles through gate in the progression exercise.

CAUTION:

Players who are inexperienced when defending will go to ground a lot. They should understand that this is the last option when defending as mistiming a sliding tackle takes the defender out of the game. Going to ground too frequently probably indicates poor positioning, lack of concentration or laziness. Players should practice getting into cover positions, tracking forward runs, and concentrating on opposition movement.

13: Screening as a Pair

PURPOSE OF SESSION:

For players to practice working in pairs with an emphasis on screening forward passes.

INITIAL SET-UP:

- Playing area is divided into thirds, with two small goals at either end.

- Two Black players are in the central zone attempting to intercept passes between White pairs.

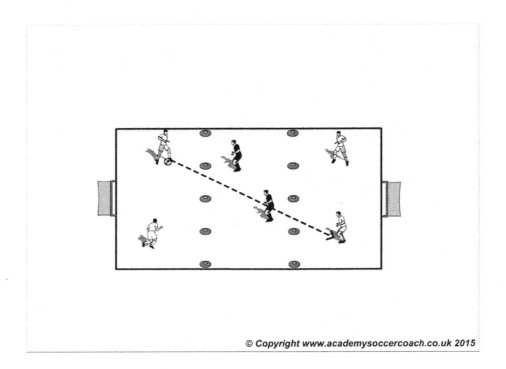

INSTRUCTIONS:

- The White attacking players attempt to pass the ball to their opposite pair. They initially should not pass over head-height.

- **TRANSITION:** When Black players intercept a pass, they can combine to score in the small goal where the pass originated.

PROGRESSIONS:

1. An opposite White attacker can drop into the central zone and passes can now be played through him, or directly to the opposite end.

2. One of the Black defenders can now leave the central zone to press the ball. The Whites can now play through the zone, using a central player or pass over the central players.

3. Can be adapted and changed into exercise 18.

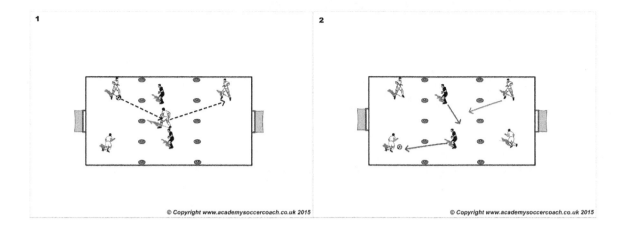

CHALLENGES / QUESTIONS FOR PLAYERS:

- Can the pair work together to discourage or intercept forward passes?

- Can they position themselves at an angle and distance where a pass cannot be played through the center of the pair?

- When an opposition White player 'drops in', can the pair both stop him receiving, turning and passing, as well as prevent direct forward passes?

- If a pass is played long and high, can the defender pressure and spoil the receiver's touch and look to intercept?

- Once possession is won back, can the defenders counter-attack and score in the opposite goal? Can you be clinical when doing so, then recover to stop the next attack?

SCORING:

Attackers receive a point for every pass they play through the central zone. They get an extra point for playing a pass that splits the defending pair. Defenders get a point for every goal they score.

CAUTION:

When a pass successfully gets through the central zone, it can disorganize defenders very quickly and they often concede further goals very quickly. Encourage them to reorganize as swiftly as possible.

14: Defending in & Around the Box

PURPOSE OF SESSION:

Defenders learn to defend critically when playing in and around the penalty area.

INITIAL SET-UP:

- Three White defenders and a goalkeeper defend the big goal.
- Three grey attackers receive from any Black server and try to score.
- Three smaller goals are positioned outside the box to allow the Whites to counter-attack.

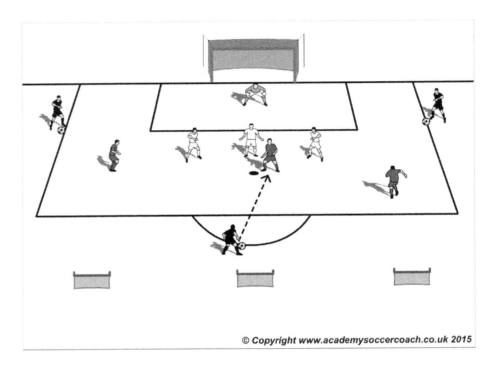

INSTRUCTIONS:

- Players play 3 v 3 in the penalty area.
- Each attack is started by one of the Black servers playing a pass into the attackers. Greys attempt to score a goal.
- **TRANSITION:** If the White defenders intercept the ball, can they score in any of the three smaller goals? Greys and Blacks must recover and defend against this.
- Switch players regularly, especially if players have been 'servers' for an extended period.

PROGRESSIONS:

1. The Black server who feeds the attacking team can now join the attack, creating an overload.
2. All three Black servers can join the attack.

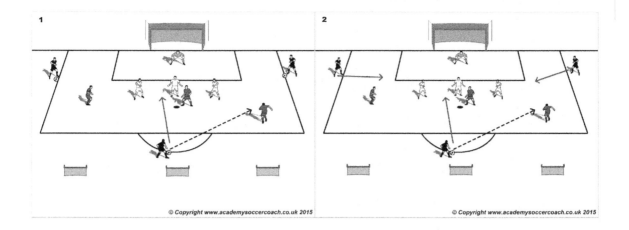

CHALLENGES / QUESTIONS FOR PLAYERS:

- Can the three defenders defend compactly?
- Can you zonally defend the goal as a priority, rather than man-marking?
- Can you detect when a player is shaping up to shoot and press the ball accordingly?
- Can defenders be alive to any rebounds that come from the goalkeeper?
- When outnumbered, can players prioritise defending the goal compactly, recognising when it is *critical* to press the ball?
- Upon regaining possession, can the White defenders counter-attack quickly?
- Can the attacking team react quickly to defend from any counter-attack?

SCORING:

Count the attacking team's score versus how many the defending team score with a counter-attack. The goalkeeper can score (with hands or feet) should he have possession.

CAUTION:

Rotate players frequently.

15: Defending when Outnumbered 2 v 3

PURPOSE OF SESSION:

Players practice and learn the Principles of Defending when Outnumbered.

INITIAL SET-UP:

- Playing area with two goals and no goalkeepers.
- Three attackers v two defenders.

INSTRUCTIONS:

- Players play 2 v 3 in the area.
- **TRANSITION:** Both teams attack and defend the goals, allowing for inherent transitions.

PROGRESSIONS:

1. Add corner zones to the area. If the defender forces an opponent into these zones, the attacker is out of bounds.

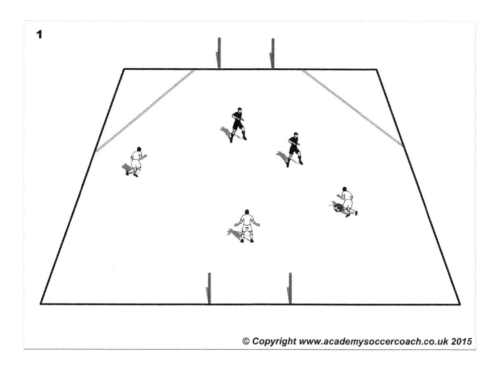

CHALLENGES / QUESTIONS FOR PLAYERS:

- Can you be patient and *delay* the attacks of opponents?

- Can you *deny* the attackers from scoring directly by manoeuvring into positions between the ball and goal?

- Can you get close enough to one player to dictate or force him away from goal?

- Can you use any opportunity to defend strongly and win the ball?

- Can you counter-attack quickly and sensibly (considering you are outnumbered and will need to recover quickly) and score a goal?

SCORING:

The number of goals scored by each team.

CAUTION:

If the defenders are finding it overly difficult to counter-attack and score, give them an extra point/goal if they force attackers out of bounds.

16: Two v Three Chaos

PURPOSE OF SESSION:

Players not only practice defending when outnumbered, they do so with lots of interference from other players.

INITIAL SET-UP:

- Two games of 2 v 3 take place simultaneously, in the same playing area.

- Two Whites v three Blacks; two stripes v three greys.

- Each team attacks and defends one small goal.

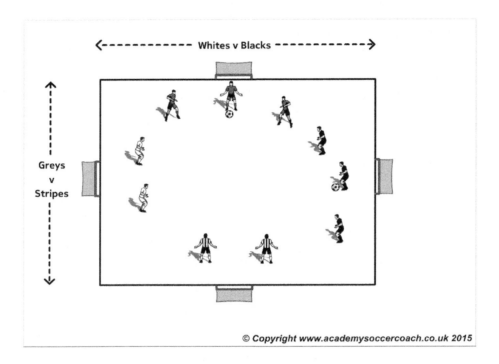

INSTRUCTIONS:

- Both games are played simultaneously for five minutes.

- Players are challenged to deal with being both outnumbered and with the interference and traffic from the other game.

- **TRANSITION:** Natural transitions occur as the ball changes hands.

PROGRESSIONS:

1. Change the teams playing against each other. Create a 'round robin' style competition.

2. Change the teams who are outnumbered.

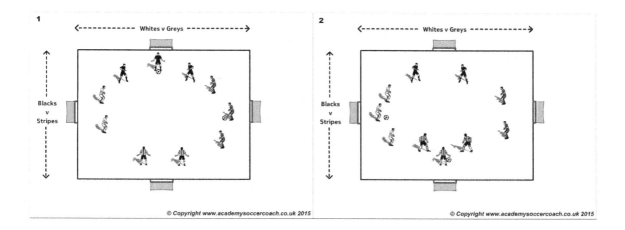

CHALLENGES / QUESTIONS FOR PLAYERS:

- Can the outnumbered team defend according to the Defending when Outnumbered Principles of Play?

- Can players make good decisions in the face of extra interference from the other game?

- Can you defend *critically* when required?

- Can you counter-attack effectively, knowing that you will be exposed if the ball transitions again?

- Can you recover and reorganize quickly to defend the goal once possession is lost?

SCORING:

Goals scored. Make a round robin competition, keeping the score of each fixture.

CAUTION:

Focus on a particular pair at one time. As the exercise is busy and chaotic, if you attempt to see everything all at once, it becomes too complicated and you end up seeing nothing!

17: Random Outnumbered

PURPOSE OF SESSION:

Players defend in several outnumbered situations.

INITIAL SET-UP:

- The playing area is divided into three zones. Each zone has a goal to attack and defend.

- Both teams have even numbers overall.

- The coach organizes three different outnumbered situations (depending on the number of players).

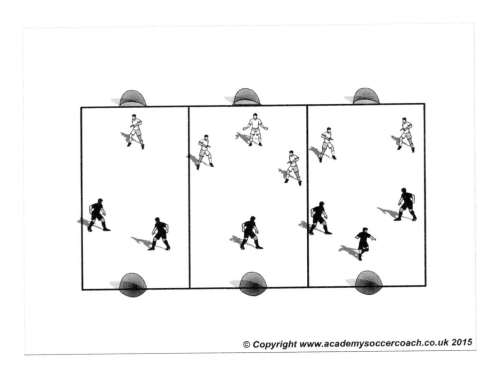

INSTRUCTIONS:

- Players play several outnumbered games simultaneously for five minutes.

- The final scores of each game are added together to give a final 'team' score. Players need to analyze when they need to score or defend, based on the other scores. For example, if the Black pair and threesome are both winning, the single Black can focus on defending.

- **TRANSITION:** Natural transitions as the ball changes hands.

- Constantly switch the players between games to give them lots of different experiences.

PROGRESSIONS:

1. Ask the Black team to choose how many players they will play in each zone. The Whites then 'react' to this and decide how many players will oppose them in each area.

2. Remove zones and players play one big game on a pitch that is wide and short.

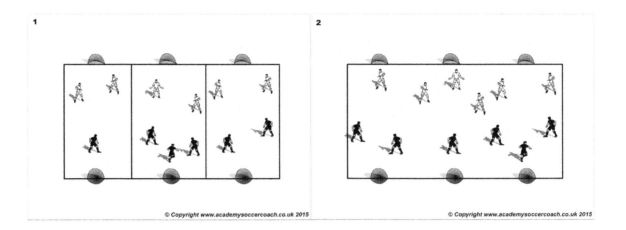

CHALLENGES / QUESTIONS FOR PLAYERS:

- Can players defend in line with the Defending when Outnumbered Principles of Play?

- Can players be aware of what the scores are on the pitches around them to make a decision about what strategy to use?

- When players regain possession, can they counter-attack to score? Can they run the clock down if necessary?

- Can players work together socially to decide on team strategy, where to place extra players, and where to defend when outnumbered?

- If you decide to completely outnumber players in one zone, what implications will that have for your teammate who may be defending alone?

SCORING:

Goals scored. The winner is the team with the most accumulated goals across all mini-games.

CAUTION:

Depending on numbers you could make four zones, etc.

Ensure players' decisions are based on a desire to win the game and will not play 3 v 1 simply to toy with or embarrass their opponent.

18: Sliding & Screening as a Unit

PURPOSE OF SESSION:

To allow a unit of players (namely a back four or midfield four) to practice being compact and sliding and screening to stop forward, penetrative passes.

INITIAL SET-UP:

- Playing area is divided into thirds, with a narrower central area.

- There is a goal at either end.

- Four players in the defensive central zone. Three to five in players in the end zones.

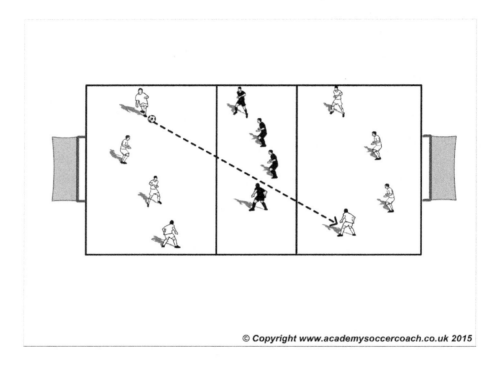

© Copyright www.academysoccercoach.co.uk 2015

INSTRUCTIONS:

- The White teams aim to penetrate the central zone by playing penetrative passes through the Black team. Passes must be below head-height to start with.

- The central screening players remain compact and intercept as many passes through the central zone as possible.

- **TRANSITION:** When the Black defenders intercept, they can attack the goal from the zone the pass came from. Whites must then recover to defend the goal.

- Switch players as necessary.

PROGRESSIONS:

1. A single Black defender can now leave the central zone at any one time to press the ball (if appropriate).

2. A single Black player can press, but the Whites can now play long over the defenders' heads.

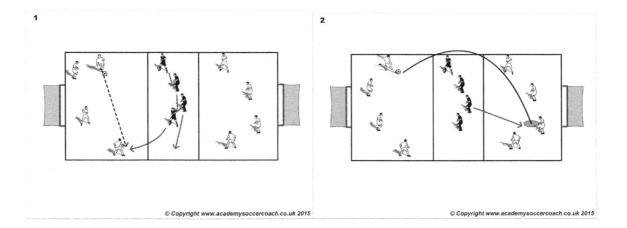

CHALLENGES / QUESTIONS FOR PLAYERS:

- Can the unit work together to discourage or intercept forward passes?

- Can they position themselves at angles and distances where a pass cannot be played through them?

- Can they work together to 'slide' as one unit to cover the most dangerous areas?

- If a pass is played long and high, can the defender pressure and spoil the receiver's touch and look to intercept?

- When one player is pressing, can he press intelligently and not just chase the ball 1 v 4? Can he isolate a player 1 v 1 or make play predictable for the defenders behind him?

- If it is inappropriate to press, can you maintain your shape and force longer passes?

- Once possession is won back, can the defenders counter-attack and score in the opposite goal? Can you be clinical when doing so, and then recover to stop the next attack?

SCORING:

The White team scores by passing through the central area, but only half a point for passing over it. Defenders get a point for intercepting and scoring a goal.

CAUTION:

Change central players as appropriate.

19: Critical Defending with Three

PURPOSE OF SESSION:

To 'stress' center-backs and a holding midfield player. They will practice defending *critically*, in and around the penalty area.

INITIAL SET-UP:

- Half a pitch set up with two goals and two target areas for Whites to score in.

- Three White players (two center-backs & holding midfielder) defend a big goal, along with the goalkeeper.

- All other players (Blacks) attack the big goal and try to score.

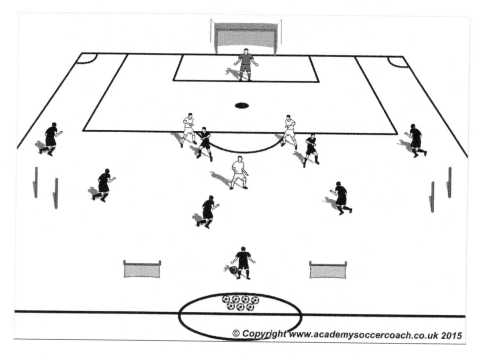

INSTRUCTIONS:

- The three White players are intentionally severely outnumbered.

- The Black team start with the ball and attempt to score a goal (put a time limit on this to encourage urgency and quick attacks to add further stress to defenders).

- The White team defend five attacks, with little or no break between attacks.

- **TRANSITION:** If the Whites or goalkeeper win the ball back, they can score in either two goals, or pass into the red gates.

PROGRESSIONS:

1. Change the three defenders and make a competition – one group against the other!

2. Progress the exercise to contain a back four and midfield two (exercise 20).

CHALLENGES / QUESTIONS FOR PLAYERS:

*   Do you have the will to defend while completely outnumbered?

*   Can you block, tackle, head, intercept while *critically* defending?

*   Can you collect rebounds from the goalkeeper?

*   Can you prioritise when to drop off and delay attacks, or when you critically need to press a shot on goal, etc, as with the Defending when Outnumbered Principles of Play.

*   If you find yourself in a 1 v 1, can you be aggressive and win the ball back?

*   When an attack breaks down, can you squeeze out quickly to clear the penalty area?

*   Are you 'alive' to transition quickly when you win the ball back?

SCORING:

Use two groups of defenders, and measure the number of clean sheets per set of five attacks.

CAUTION:

Work in short bursts, but make it really intense before resting. Once one attack ends, start another. The attack only comes to an end if they break the time limit or the ball goes out of play. The game is still alive even if the ball ends up in the goalkeeper's hands.

20: Critical Defending with Six

PURPOSE OF SESSION:

To 'stress' a back four and two holding midfielders. They are required to practice defending whilst disorganized and *critically*, in and around the penalty area.

INITIAL SET-UP:

- Half a pitch set up with two goals and two target areas for Whites to score in.

- A back four and two screening midfielders defend a big goal, along with the goalkeeper.

- All other players (Blacks) attack the big goal and try to score.

INSTRUCTIONS:

- Try to outnumber the six players as much as possible. Use only one midfielder if that helps facilitate this.

- The Black team start with the ball and attempt to score a goal (put a time limit on this to encourage urgency and quick attacks to further stress players).

- The White team defend in five-minute blocks, with little or no break between attacks.

- **TRANSITION:** If the Whites or goalkeeper win the ball back, they can score in either of the two goals, or pass into the red gates.

PROGRESSIONS:

1. Whites score double if any player can run the ball through either gate. The player must, however, recover (transition) quickly.

2. Regress the exercise so that just three (plus goalkeeper) are defending (exercise 19).

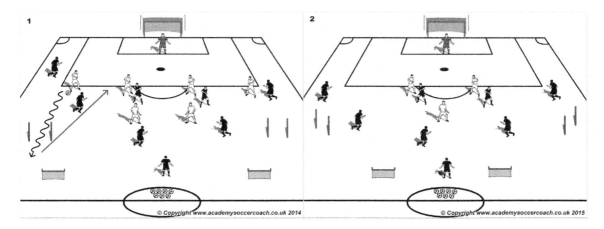

CHALLENGES / QUESTIONS FOR PLAYERS:

- Do you have the will to defend while completely out-numbered?

- Can you critically defend when chances on goal occur?

- Can defenders react more quickly than strikers to rebounds or potential rebounds from the goalkeeper?

- Can you prioritize when to drop off, delay attacks and force passes wide / sideways, or when you critically need to press a shot on goal etc. as per the Defending when Outnumbered Principles of Play?

- If you find yourself in a 1 v 1, can you be aggressive and win the ball back?

- When an attack breaks down, can you squeeze out quickly to clear the penalty area?

- Are you 'alive' to transition quickly when you win the ball back?

SCORING:

Count goals of Blacks versus goals of White. It can actually be harder for the attacking team to score in the big goal, so give a further incentive to Blacks if necessary – e.g. a goal is worth five. This also challenges the defenders further, knowing that one goal conceded can have a huge impact on the score line.

CAUTION:

Change players in and out of the defending team to allow physical and mental rest.

Position-Specific Defending

The following ten exercises look at defending, but now have a much more specific outcome in terms of players' positions.

We will, of course, spend lots of time coaching defending to defensive-minded players, but there are simultaneous outcomes for players who play in attacking positions also. Remember, in today's game, very few players, if any, are *just* attackers or *just* defenders. They are both. All players attack and defend, and all need to be able to transition between both.

Even though these practices are now focused on certain positions, pairings and units, it is important that you do not neglect the defensive outcomes of the remaining players involved. Encourage a high level of defending and a high level of defensive transition.

21: Centre-Backs Defending Box

PURPOSE OF SESSION:

For a center-back pairing to defend effectively in and around the penalty area.

INITIAL SET-UP:

- Two center-backs and goalkeeper versus two strikers in the penalty box.

- Four feeders playing with the attacking team.

- Four gated goals set up around the edge of the box.

INSTRUCTIONS:

- Feeders take it in turns to pass balls into strikers for them to score a goal. Defenders and goalkeeper look to stop strikers scoring.

- **TRANSITION:** Once defenders regain possession, they must dribble through any of the gated goals. They must then recover quickly as the Blacks mount another attack.

PROGRESSIONS:

1. Feeders can now pass the ball between them before passing into the strikers, meaning the center-backs will constantly need to adjust their position to deal with the location of the ball and the movement of the strikers.

2. Once a pass is played into the strikers, any of the feeders can join the attack.

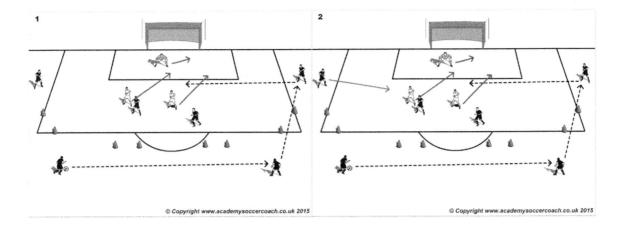

CHALLENGES / QUESTIONS FOR PLAYERS:

- When should you mark tightly and when should you mark loosely?
- Can you mentally and physically track the movement of strikers?
- How does the movement of the ball between feeders change your position?
- Can you constantly adjust your position to stop the opposition from scoring?
- Can you 'spoil' the strikers' first touches?
- Can you defend *critically* when the strikers are in a position to shoot?

SCORING:

Attackers score by scoring in the big goal. The defending team scores by counter-attacking through the orange gates.

CAUTION:

Do not accept center-backs being 'lazy' and not adjusting their position. Encourage feeders to punish this laziness with clinical passes to score.

22: Defending Crosses

PURPOSE OF SESSION:

For players, particularly center-backs and goalkeepers, to practice defending from crosses and the movements of strikers.

INITIAL SET-UP:

- Two goals with goalkeepers on a small-sided pitch.

- Two Black players act as wingers who produce crosses for two strikers to attack.

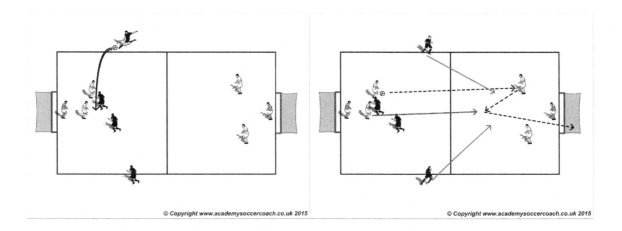

© Copyright www.academysoccercoach.co.uk 2015   © Copyright www.academysoccercoach.co.uk 2015

INSTRUCTIONS:

- Each goal is defended by two center-backs and a goalkeeper.

- The practice starts with one of the wide players receiving a pass before playing a cross into the goal area for the attackers to attempt to score.

- Defenders look to defend the goal – the first taking his position in line with the near post, the other in the middle of the goal.

- **TRANSITION:** As per diagram two, above, if a defender wins the ball, can he play quickly into the opposite White player who sets up a shot for his defensive partner. The Black wide players must recover quickly to transition, and the Whites must quickly reorganize after attacking.

- Once one attack ends, the opposite wide player attacks and strikers attack the other goal.

PROGRESSIONS:

1. The opposite wide player can also attack the cross to try and score, forcing the center-backs to defend 2 v 3.

2. When in possession, the Black attackers can switch the goal they intend to score in. They must, however, pass wide and attempt to score from a cross.

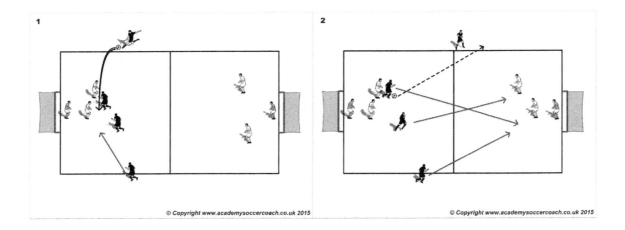

CHALLENGES / QUESTIONS FOR PLAYERS:

- Can you defend with an 'open body' position (i.e. able to see both the ball being crossed and the closest attacking player)?

- Can the two centre-backs drop back, or step up, depending on the position of the crosser?

- Can the first defender look to defend in line with the front post?

- Can the second defender take up a position in the middle of the goal?

- Can defenders move their feet quickly to adjust their position if necessary?

- Can defenders see and track the movement of the attackers?

- Can the goalkeeper command his area both vocally and come and catch / punch any crosses and help take pressure off his center-backs?

- Can the Whites counter-attack quickly once they regain the ball?

- Can Black players recover quickly should the Whites begin to counter-attack?

SCORING:

Only goals count – how many can the Black attackers score v. the White defenders?

Encourage competition between center-back pairings by counting how many goals they concede.

CAUTION:

Ensure there is a 'flow' to the exercise by having lots of spare balls and moving attacks between goals promptly.

23: Back 4 Compact

PURPOSE OF SESSION:

To allow defenders in a back four to defend as a unit, defend compactly, and prioritize what areas to defend.

INITIAL SET-UP:

- Whites v. Blacks play in the playing area, 4 v 4.

- The pitch is short and wide.

- Each team defends three small goals.

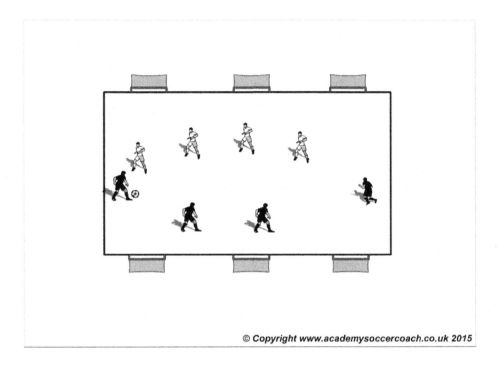

INSTRUCTIONS:

- Players play 4v4 in the area. When out of possession, players must cover the goals that are under most threat.

- **TRANSITION:** This exercise is an adaptation of a small-sided game so natural transitions occur as the ball changes hands.

PROGRESSIONS:

1. Add extra players to one team to 'stress' defenders further.

2. The two added players could play as attacking 'floaters' – playing only for the team in possession.

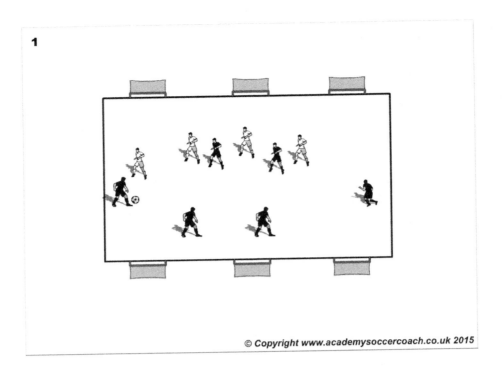

CHALLENGES / QUESTIONS FOR PLAYERS:

- Can you work together to defend the goal or goals that are most under threat?

- Can you ensure that the spaces between the back four do not allow for a penetrative pass?

- Can you adjust your collective positions to shift across the pitch as the opposition changes the point of attack?

- When the ball is central, can you cover a clear shot to all three of the goals?

- Can you counter-attack and score quickly against a disorganized opponent?

- Once your attack has ended, can you recover quickly to stop counter-attacks and reorganize?

SCORING:

Count the goals as per any small-sided game.

CAUTION:

When out of possession, ensure each team is defending as a back four, rather than changing the team's formation. Temporary changes are acceptable but ensure the aim of players is to recover into their defensive shape.

24: Defending Against Direct Play

PURPOSE OF SESSION:

To allow a defensive unit to practice defending against direct play and, in particular, the space in behind them.

INITIAL SET-UP:

- Two areas are set up – a possession zone and a scoring / defending zone.

- A back four (or three, or five) take up their defensive line on the edge of the scoring / defending zone.

- It is very useful to have two coaches – one to manage the possession zone, one to manage the defenders.

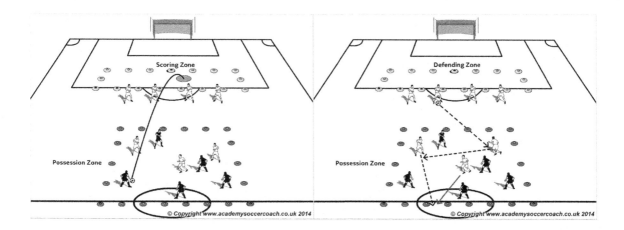

INSTRUCTIONS:

- Blacks outnumber Whites in the possession zone.

- Blacks attempt to play a long pass that lands in the scoring zone.

- The Whites in the possession zone and back four players try to stop them from scoring.

- **TRANSITION:** If the Whites win possession, they try to get the ball to the end line (diagram 2).

PROGRESSIONS:

1. When Whites are in *good* possession, the back four can disperse and they can score by running over the halfway line. However, as a unit they must recover quickly into defensive shape (transition) upon scoring or losing the ball.

2. Add two strikers. Blacks can now play to strikers' feet, who score if they manoeuvre their way into the scoring zone. Blacks can still play a long pass in behind to the scoring zone. Whites can still disperse when in possession.

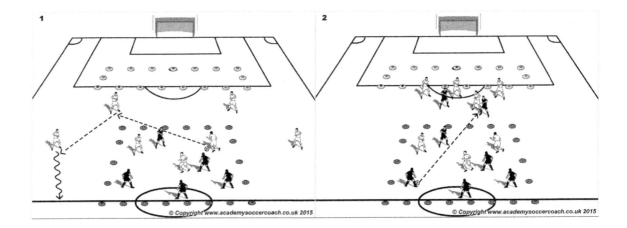

CHALLENGES / QUESTIONS FOR PLAYERS:

- Can the back four move laterally as the ball moves around the possession zone?

- Can you pick up the visual cues of when a Black player is going to try a long pass in behind the defence?

- When a teammate is going to head / control the ball, can the other three players narrow off and cover behind him?

- Can you quickly 'squeeze' out of the scoring zone once the danger has passed?

- Can you recover quickly into shape when possession is lost?

- Can you stop strikers turning, or spoil the passes into their feet?

- Can you counter-attack effectively and reorganize once disorganized?

SCORING:

Blacks score by playing into the scoring zone. The White back four defends for 3 to 4 minutes – how many goals did they prevent? Whites also score by stopping the ball on the end line.

CAUTION:

Use a second coach, if possible, to manage the possession zone. Ensure you rotate the players who are outnumbered.

25: Outnumbered In / Around Box

PURPOSE OF SESSION:

For a back four to defend while outnumbered and keep attackers out of the goal area.

INITIAL SET-UP:

- Back four plus goalkeeper versus six attackers.
- Place four gates across the width of the box and four gates near the halfway line facing them.

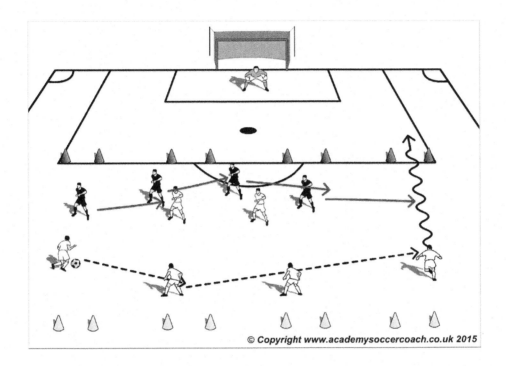

INSTRUCTIONS:

- White attackers start with the ball and attack the big goal. They must first dribble or pass the ball through an orange gate before scoring.

- Black defenders must stop attackers from entering the penalty area. If the attackers do get into the area, they can score unopposed against the goalkeeper.

- **TRANSITION:** If the defenders win the ball back, they can dribble through the opposite yellow gates. The scorer must then recover quickly to stop the Whites countering the counter-attack.

PROGRESSIONS:

1. Defenders can now enter the penalty area to defend. Their first task is to keep opponents out of the box, then stop them scoring.

2. Introduce goals rather than gates for the defenders to counter-attack into.

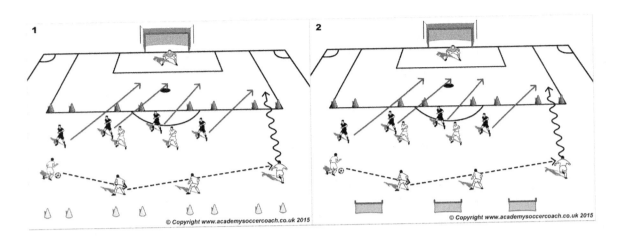

CHALLENGES / QUESTIONS FOR PLAYERS:

- Can you be patient and *delay* the attacks of the opponents?

- When the ball switches from one side to the other, can you 'travel as the ball travels', while remaining compact?

- Can you *deny* the attackers from scoring directly by manoeuvring into positions between the ball and targets?

- Can you get close enough to one player to *dictate* or force him away from goal?

- Can you use any opportunity to defend strongly and win the ball?

- Once the attackers are in the box, can you defend *critically* and stop them scoring?

- Can you counter-attack quickly and sensibly (considering you are outnumbered and will need to recover quickly) and score a goal?

SCORING:

Attackers get a point for scoring a goal, defenders get a point for dribbling through a yellow gate or scoring in one of the smaller goals.

CAUTION:

Adjust the size of the gates if the challenge is proving too difficult / too easy.

26: Sweeper

PURPOSE OF SESSION:

Introduce players to the role of the sweeper in covering teammates when the opposition break through. Can also be used for defensive midfielders.

INITIAL SET-UP:

- Whites v. Blacks play in the larger central playing area.

- A 'sweeper' from each team is confined to the final thirds.

- Each team has three gated goals to attack and defend.

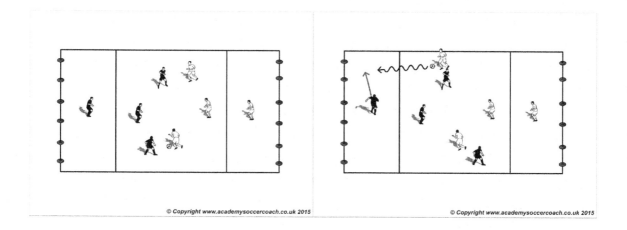

INSTRUCTIONS:

- Play starts with even teams in the central zone. Players can shoot and attempt to score from this central area. Only attackers, however, can leave this zone and enter the final third (by dribbling or receiving a pass) occupied by the sweeper.

- The sweeper at each end must read dangerous attacks and spoil the opposition scoring a goal. He can do this by screening longer shots, or by tackling / intercepting players that enter the area to score.

- **TRANSITION:** If the sweeper wins possession, he can set up an attack by passing forward to teammates.

PROGRESSIONS:

1. When in possession, the sweeper can now enter the central zone to join in the attacks and outnumber the opposition. He must quickly drop back, however, if there is a transition. Even when in possession he must concentrate and consider his position if his team loses the ball.

2. Add goals and goalkeepers.

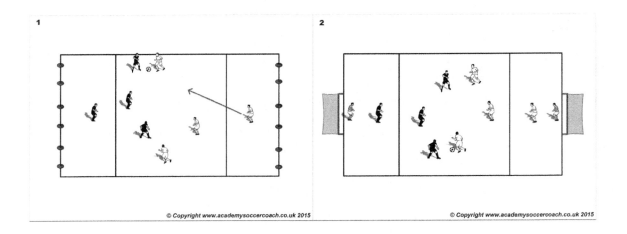

CHALLENGES / QUESTIONS FOR PLAYERS:

- How many forward passes can the sweeper screen?

- Can the sweeper read impending danger and position himself to deal with it?

- Can the sweeper alter his position as the play builds? Be *pro*-active in sensing danger, rather than *re*-acting to a dangerous situation.

- Can the sweeper block, tackle and intercept attacks as necessary?

- If the sweeper joins in the attack, is he always aware of readjusting his position to stop the opponent from counter-attacking quickly, and scoring?

- Can you communicate to your teammates about their position, the tracking of forward runs, screening of passes etc?

SCORING:

Both teams score by passing or dribbling through any of the three gates.

CAUTION:

Sweepers should not just stand there while the play is building up. They should always be concentrating and making slight adjustments to their position as the danger unfolds.

27: Screening Forward Passes

PURPOSE OF SESSION:

To allow players to practice screening forward passes. It is particularly useful for a midfield player who may be looking to intercept passes into strikers.

INITIAL SET-UP:

- Whites v. Blacks play in the playing area.

- A midfield screener from each team plays in a zone between the goals and playing area.

- This game can also be played with a goalkeeper defending a goal at one end, and a screener defending two.

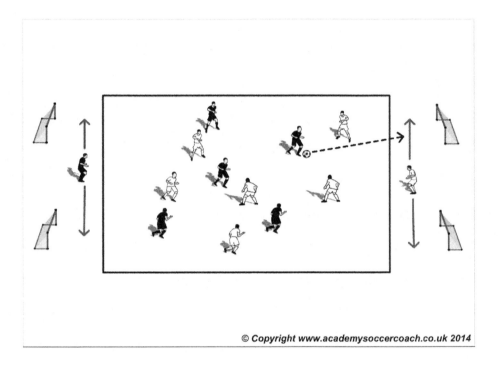

© Copyright www.academysoccercoach.co.uk 2014

INSTRUCTIONS:

- Players play 5v5 / 6v6 etc. in the playing area. A goal is scored by passing into one of the two goals being defended by the screener.

- The screening player must intercept as many goal-bound passes as he can.

- **TRANSITION:** This exercise is an adaptation of a small-sided game so natural transitions occur as the ball changes hands.

- Switch defending players as necessary.

PROGRESSIONS:

1. The screening player can now enter the main playing area to challenge if he feels he a) has no choice to prevent a goal, or b) feels he can win the ball (note how in diagram one, he arcs his run to protect the goal). If he leaves this area, he can be replaced by a teammate. Let the player decide whether they keep these roles or change back when it is safe to do so.

2. The attacking team can now leave the playing area to attack the goal, either with a dribble or an off-the-ball run. Use the end line as an offside line to ensure players time their runs and don't just stand in the goal area. The screener will protect one goal and rely on his teammate to recover and track the attacker's forward run.

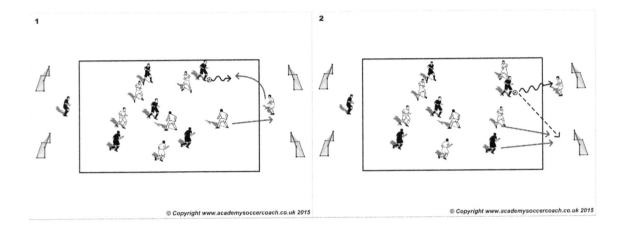

CHALLENGES / QUESTIONS FOR PLAYERS:

*   How many forward passes can you screen?

*   How many attacks can you start, having intercepted the ball?

*   When might you stay in your screening position? When might you leave it?

*   If you can leave your screening post to win the ball, was it the right decision?

*   Can your teammates contribute to your challenges by covering your position or tracking other forward runners?

*   Can you prioritize which goal to defend in certain circumstances?

SCORING:

Count the score in the game and the individual interception scores of each screener.

CAUTION:

Ensure you change the screener as appropriate.

28: Screening/Spoiling Forward Passes

PURPOSE OF SESSION:

To allow players to practice screening forward passes, and 'spoiling' their opponent's first touch.

INITIAL SET-UP:

- Whites v. Blacks play in the inner playing area.

- Two Black target players play on the end lines.

- Two White screeners play between the playing area and target players.

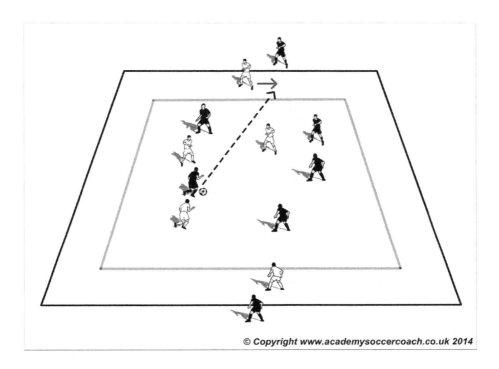

© Copyright www.academysoccercoach.co.uk 2014

INSTRUCTIONS:

- Players play 3v5 / 4v6 etc in the inner playing area, with the Whites outnumbered.

- Whites pass to their screening player to score. Blacks pass to target players to score.

- The White screening players must intercept as many forward passes as they can.

- **TRANSITION:** This exercise is an adaptation of a small-sided game so natural transitions occur as the ball changes hands.

- Switch players as necessary.

PROGRESSIONS:

1. If the Blacks play into the target player successfully, the White screener can turn and attempt to spoil his first touch, or stop him playing back to his teammates (like a midfield player defending in front of a striker).

2. If the Whites play a pass into the screener, the Black player can press from behind and try to spoil his first touch (like a center-back pressing a striker).

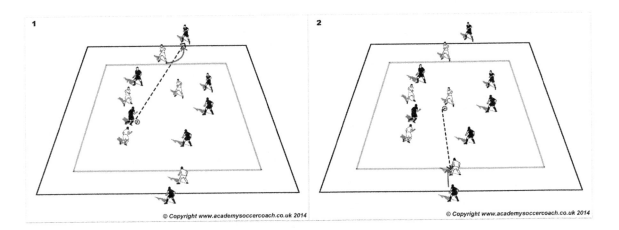

CHALLENGES / QUESTIONS FOR PLAYERS:

- How many forward passes can you screen?

- How many attacks can you start having intercepted the ball?

- If the pass does go past you, can you react and spoil the target player's first touch, or stop him playing (progression 1)?

- Black target player – can you travel as the ball travels and spoil White's first touch (Progression 2)?

- Can players playing inside the inner square stop forward passes?

- Can all players counter-attack effectively once they regain possession?

SCORING:

A goal is scored every time a team plays a pass into their target / screener. Extra point for players who spoil their first touches.

CAUTION:

Whites are out-numbered as it is theoretically easier for them to score. The coach will need to manage this by rotating the players who are outnumbered.

29: Screen Passes into Striker

PURPOSE OF SESSION:

As a unit, players practice and focus on screening passes from opponents into the striker's feet.

INITIAL SET-UP:

- The area is split into two zones.

- Four Whites v four Blacks in the larger zone.

- One striker is placed unopposed in the smaller end zone.

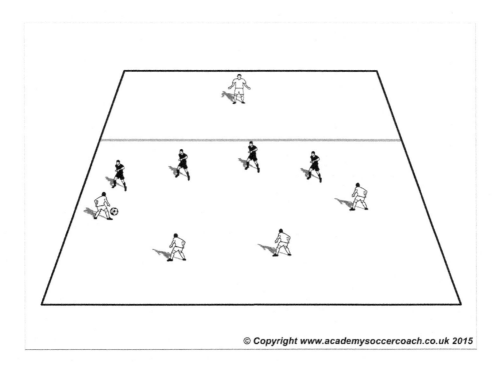

© Copyright www.academysoccercoach.co.uk 2015

INSTRUCTIONS:

- The White foursome attempt to play passes from the playing area into the White striker. This exercise works best if the Whites have to keep the ball below head height.

- Blacks are asked to stop this from happening by pressing and screening forward passes.

- **TRANSITION:** If the Black team regain possession, they can score by stopping the ball on the end line.

PROGRESSIONS:

1. Outnumber the defenders further to add extra 'stress' to their challenge.

2. Add a second striker and another defender to the end zone. The Whites can now play over head height and the defender attempts to 'spoil' the strikers' first touches.

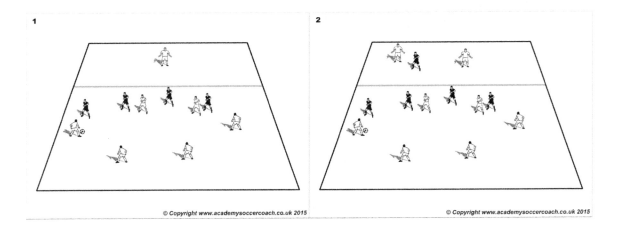

CHALLENGES / QUESTIONS FOR PLAYERS:

- How many forward passes can you screen?

- Can you slide across the pitch as a unit to stop direct forward passes?

- Can you press the ball when appropriate and regain possession?

- When outnumbered, can you work within the Defending when Outnumbered Principles of Play?

- Can you force passes sideways?

- Can you isolate an opponent 1 v 1 and be aggressive to regain the ball?

- Can the angles and distances between defenders stop Whites from playing through the Black team?

- If you regain possession, can you counter-attack effectively?

- Having counter-attacked, can you recover and reorganize quickly?

SCORING:

Whites score by successfully playing a pass into the striker. Blacks by counter-attacking and stopping the ball on the end line.

CAUTION:

Rotate the role of the lone striker.

30: Defending from the Front

PURPOSE OF SESSION:

An exercise with an emphasis on a front three pressuring the ball and stopping forward passes.

INITIAL SET-UP:

- Four defenders versus three attackers in each half.

- A halfway line divides the pitch with a 'V'-shaped zone towards the sidelines.

- Each team attacks and defends a small goal with gates either side.

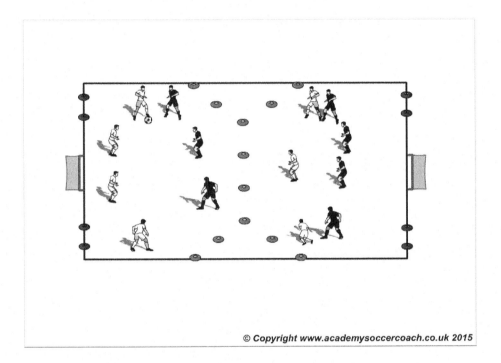

INSTRUCTIONS:

- A back four from each team plays against a front three from each team. Both groups are confined to their half.

- The back four attempts to play passes into the front three to score a goal.

- **TRANSITION:** Players who regain possession can either score in the small goal or dribble through the blue gates.

PROGRESSIONS:

1. When in possession, members of the front three can drop into the 'V' zone unopposed. The defending front three must stop passes going into these areas, and also stop passes into the central striker.

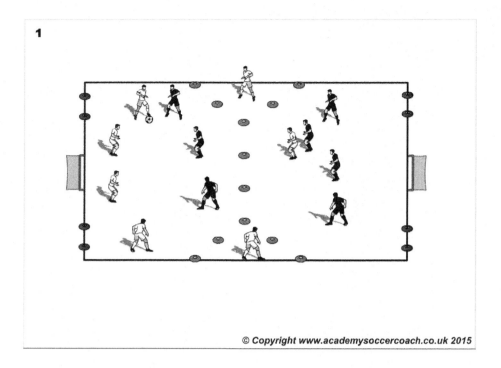

CHALLENGES / QUESTIONS FOR PLAYERS:

- Even though outnumbered, can you press and win the ball?
- When would you drop off rather than press?
- How many forward passes can you screen?
- Can you stop passes going into the unopposed 'V' area?
- Can you recognize when to press slow, poor or long, high passes and spoil the receiver's touch?
- If you regain possession, can you react quickly to score or dribble through a scoring gate?

SCORING:

A goal is scored by either scoring in the big goal or by dribbling through either of the side gates.

CAUTION:

Although the focus is on the front three players, ensure that all players defend appropriately.

Single-Sided Games

The final section is this book is the largest, and intentionally so. Small-sided games reflect the 'real' game more closely than any other exercises, so they are the acid test for your players and how they defend. While smaller group or 1 v 1 exercises can be easier to organize, control and identify problems in, it is within small-sided games where real learning, real decisions, and real coaching takes place.

The final six small-sided games are scenario-based games, where the teams are given a particular set of circumstances to overcome to win the game. These types of games can be particularly useful as they have a scoreline attached, and there will be a winner or loser based on the scenario.

31: High Pressing SSG

PURPOSE OF SESSION:

Players practice pressing opponents in advanced areas to win the ball back.

INITIAL SET-UP:

- Whites v. Blacks play 9 v 9 on a relevant sized pitch.

- Each team adopts a 3-3-2 formation.

- Two goals and two goalkeepers as normal.

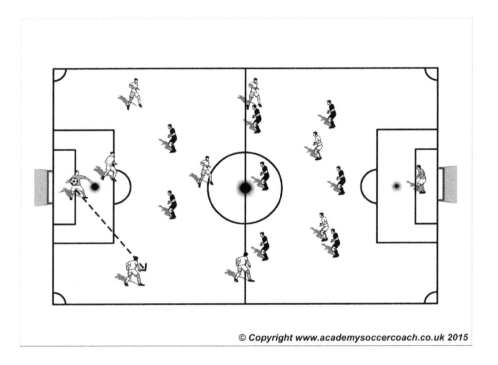

INSTRUCTIONS:

- Focus your coaching on one team, the Black team in the visual above. At first, encourage them to press high when the goalkeeper is distributing.

- Initially, simply ask the Black team to take risks and press with the single aim of regaining the ball.

- The White team are encouraged to play out from the goalkeeper through their back three.

- **TRANSITION:** Natural transitions occur in small-sided games.

PROGRESSIONS:

1. The first defender dictates play by showing the opposition full-back wide. The rest of the team mark, cover and become compact as shown, either intercepting a long forward pass,

74

'spoiling' the touch of the opponent, or regaining the ball in a duel.

2. The first defender 'shows nothing' or dictates the full-back to pass sideways. Here his strike partner plays an important role to 'travel as the ball travels' to either press the center-back, or to spoil a longer pass to the opposite full-back.

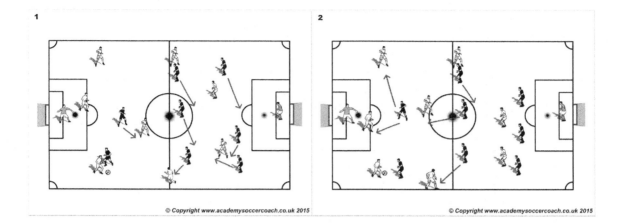

© Copyright www.academysoccercoach.co.uk 2015   © Copyright www.academysoccercoach.co.uk 2015

CHALLENGES / QUESTIONS FOR PLAYERS:

- Can the first defender get pressure on the ball?

- Can he deflect the opponent into a specific area?

- Can the rest of the team react and set up behind him according to the Defending Principles of Play?

- Can you recognize times where you are unable to press high and drop and delay the attack instead?

- If the team becomes disorganized or the opponents break through the press (which they will on occasion), can you reorganize quickly?

- Once possession is regained, can you mount a counter-attack?

SCORING:

Goals scored as normal.

CAUTION:

The premise of pressing high is like any other defending philosophy – it cannot happen 100% the way you want it *all the time*.

32: Press or Drop SSG

PURPOSE OF SESSION:

Players are encouraged to make decisions on whether to press the ball, or drop off and delay the attack.

INITIAL SET-UP:

- Whites v. Blacks play in the playing area.

- A goalkeeper defends the big goal for the White team. There is a small goal without a goalkeeper at the opposite end.

- The pitch is divided in half. A White player is offside if he is in the Black half and beyond the last defender when the ball is played.

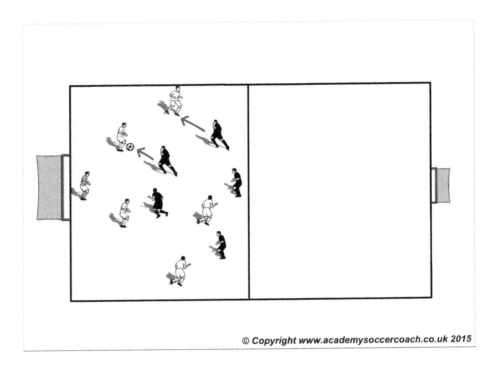

INSTRUCTIONS:

- Players play 5v5 / 6v6 etc. in the playing area – any player can move anywhere on the pitch, but the offside rule must be adhered to.

- Challenge the White team to score a goal, working within the identified rules.

- Challenge the Black team to press high, giving the Whites few forward passing options.

- **TRANSITION:** Natural transitions occur in small-sided games.

PROGRESSIONS:

1. Rather than press high, can the Black team defend deep to protect their goal?
2. Add a goalkeeper and ask the Black team to make in-game decisions about whether they should press high or drop deep.

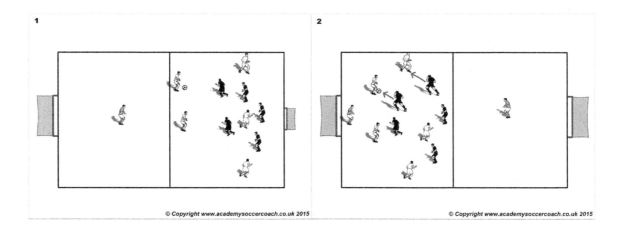

© Copyright www.academysoccercoach.co.uk 2015   © Copyright www.academysoccercoach.co.uk 2015

CHALLENGES / QUESTIONS FOR PLAYERS:

- Can the Blacks work as a team to either press or drop?
- Can players take their defending cues off the reaction of the first defender?
- If pressing high, can the Black team stop the Whites either scoring directly, or entering the space behind them?
- Can the team become compact around the ball or the goal, deflecting opponents into less dangerous areas?
- Can you defend *critically* when you are required to?
- If you regain possession, can you attack quickly and decisively, but regain defensive organization in case the Whites 'counter the counter-attack'?
- When the goalkeeper is involved, can he have a high start position when pressing and a deep one when defending deep?

SCORING:

Goals scored as normal.

CAUTION:

The most important aspect here is that all players work to the same strategy, at the same time.

33: Defending Deep SSG

PURPOSE OF SESSION:

Players defend as a team and attempt to defend deep and compact.

INITIAL SET-UP:

- Whites v. Blacks play in the playing area, which is divided into thirds.

- Black defending team is outnumbered.

- A goalkeeper defends one big goal along with the defending team. Two target players are confined to an area at the opposite end.

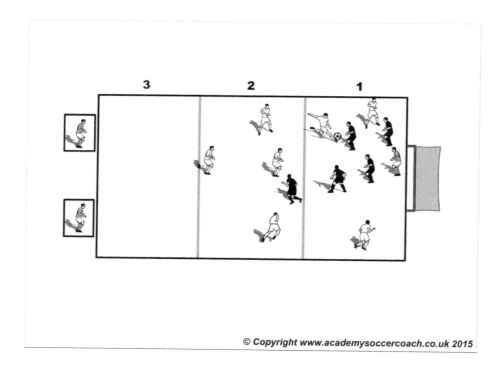

© Copyright www.academysoccercoach.co.uk 2015

INSTRUCTIONS:

- Although the pitch is split into thirds, there is no restriction on where players can move.

- The attacking White team can only score when in zone 1.

- As they are outnumbered, the defending team should (generally) retreat to stop the Whites from entering zone 1.

- **TRANSITION:** This exercise is an adaptation of a small-sided game so natural transitions occur as the ball changes hands.

PROGRESSIONS:

1. Challenge the defending team to score from counter-attacks with a pass from a specific zone – for example, a direct pass from zone 1, several short passes to score from zone 2 or run with the ball to score from zone 3.

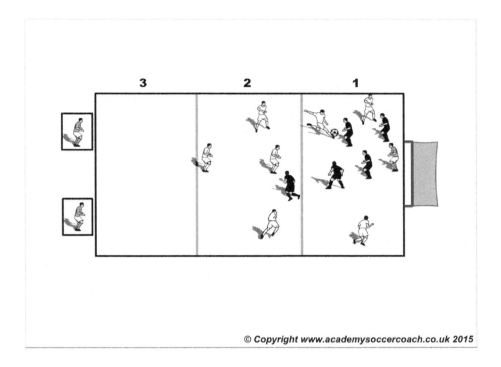

CHALLENGES / QUESTIONS FOR PLAYERS:

- Can you drop back, defend compactly and not allow the White team access to zone 1?

- As you are outnumbered, can you prioritize when to press the ball, when to drop, when to mark a player tightly, or when to mark space?

- When under threat in zone 1, can you defend *critically* to deny the Whites a scoring opportunity?

- Can you regain possession and counter-attack swiftly and effectively?

SCORING:

Whites score in the big goal, Blacks by getting the ball to the target players. Depending on what the coach wants to work on, he can award more points for a counter-attacking goal from a specific zone.

CAUTION:

Target players are confined to a small area, therefore the quality of pass forward should allow them to control the ball, rather than encouraging defenders to play aimless, long passes forward.

34: Forcing Play into Wide Areas

PURPOSE OF SESSION:

To encourage players to force or deflect attacks into wide areas and away from goal.

INITIAL SET-UP:

- Whites v. Blacks on a small-sided pitch.

- Two goalkeepers defend two goals as normal.

- Four areas are created in the corners. A player is out of bounds if forced into this area.

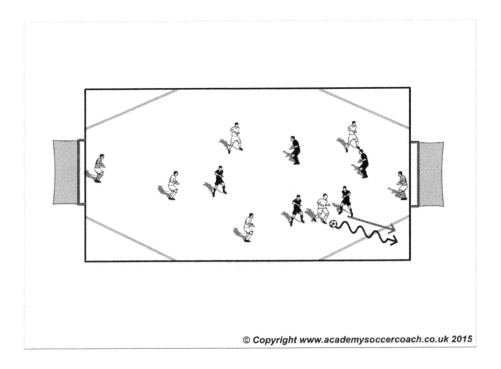

© Copyright www.academysoccercoach.co.uk 2015

INSTRUCTIONS:

- Players play 5v5 / 6v6 etc. in playing area.

- Challenge players on both teams to force opponents away from goal into the wide zones (where appropriate).

- **TRANSITION:** Natural transitions occur in small-sided games.

PROGRESSIONS:

1. Omit the corner areas and see if defenders can deflect attacks out of play (when appropriate), or at least force them into wider, less dangerous areas.

© Copyright www.academysoccercoach.co.uk 2015

CHALLENGES / QUESTIONS FOR PLAYERS:

- When appropriate, can you force or deflect an opponent away from goal?

- Can you force him out of bounds?

- Although forcing play is the focus, can you defend appropriately at all other times?

- Can you work within the Defending Principles of Play, defending *critically*, counter-attacking and recovering as necessary?

SCORING:

Goals scored as normal.

CAUTION:

Ensure the game condition of forcing players into an out of bounds area doesn't detract from players making good decisions. For example, allowing a winger to dribble past to 'create' the opportunity to force him out. This creates fake decisions.

35: Force Play Into Wide Areas

PURPOSE OF SESSION:

To encourage players to force or 'deflect' the opposition into wide areas and away from goal, and keeping them in those areas if possible.

INITIAL SET-UP:

- Whites v. Blacks play in a playing area that is split into thirds length-ways.

- Two goals, two even teams, and two goalkeepers.

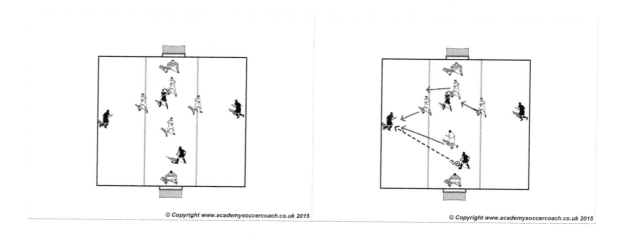

INSTRUCTIONS:

- Players play a small-sided game as normal. Although the pitch is divided into thirds, players can still move anywhere within the area.

- The White team (out of possession) look to form a block to discourage a direct central attack towards goal, and therefore force the play into wide areas.

- **TRANSITION:** Natural transitions occur in small-sided games.

CHALLENGES / QUESTIONS FOR PLAYERS:

- How can we block off attacks in central areas?

- Can we deflect the opposition into the wide areas?

- Once in wide areas, can we confine them in those areas until we regain possession, or force them out of play?

- Can you stop a tricky opponent dribbling from a wide area into goal-scoring areas?

- Can the rest of the team act as cover and balance players should the attacking team dribble out of the wide area?

- Can we ensure the team is compact and give the opposition limited passing options out of the wide channel?

- Can you regain possession and counter-attack quickly and efficiently?

SCORING:

Goals scored by both teams.

CAUTION:

When encouraged to confine attackers to wide areas, players often focus on cutting off the route back to the center *only*. Remember, the first priority here is to stop players from playing into attacking areas near the goal.

36: Defending Compact Phase of Play

PURPOSE OF SESSION:

For players to focus on defending compactly in tactical situations.

INITIAL SET-UP:

- Eight Whites (plus goalkeeper) v nine attacking players on 2/3 of a full pitch.

- Blacks attack one big goal; Whites attack three small goals.

- Divide the pitch into five zones as shown.

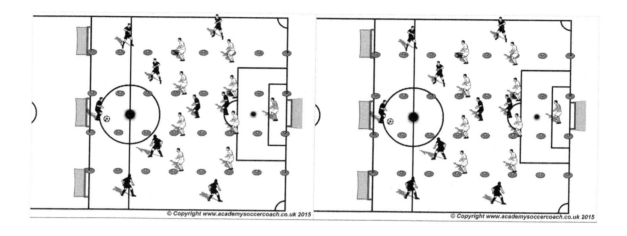

INSTRUCTIONS:

- Blacks attack as necessary to attempt to score a goal.

- Any player can move anywhere within the playing area.

- When out of possession, the White team is encouraged to position themselves across three of the five zones. The formation they choose should reflect the team's formation.

- **TRANSITION:** Once the Whites regain possession, they attempt to counter-attack and score in any of the three small goals.

PROGRESSIONS:

1. Set up with a team playing 4-5-1 or 4-3-3 compactly.
2. Set up with a team playing 3-5-2 compactly.

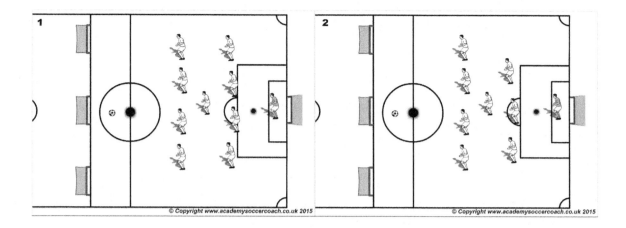

CHALLENGES / QUESTIONS FOR PLAYERS:

- When out of possession, can the team occupy the three zones where the most danger exists (i.e. where the ball is)?

- Can units slide and screen forward passes as the play switches sides?

- Can players force attacks into the less dangerous wide areas?

- Can the compactness of the team stop the opposition playing over or through the defence?

- Can players stop forward passes or spoil the touch of players receiving a forward pass?

- Can players communicate effectively?

- Can players *critically* defend when required?

- Once the team has counter-attacked, can they transition quickly to recover and re-compact?

SCORING:

Blacks score against the goalkeeper in the big goal. Whites score in any of the three smaller goals.

CAUTION:

Encourage the defending team to counter-attack with ambition. By doing this they will disorganize themselves and will be challenged to work hard to recover, reorganize and re-compact.

37: Defending in Wide Areas

PURPOSE OF SESSION:

To allow players to practice defending in wide areas, and defending subsequent crosses.

INITIAL SET-UP:

- Whites v. Blacks play in the playing area.

- Two channels are in place in the wide areas. One player from each team is allowed to enter these channels.

- Two goalkeepers defend two goals as normal.

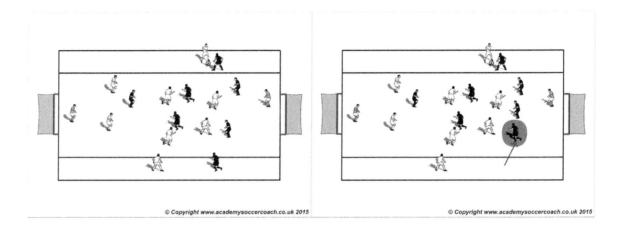

© Copyright www.academysoccercoach.co.uk 2015   © Copyright www.academysoccercoach.co.uk 2015

INSTRUCTIONS:

- Players play 5v5 / 6v6 etc. in playing area.

- Both teams are allowed only one player in each channel.

- When defending an attack from the opposite side of the pitch, the defending full-back can 'tuck in' and be compact with his other defenders.

- **TRANSITION:** Natural transitions occur in small-sided games.

PROGRESSIONS:

1. If the attack is being built down one channel, a second attacker and defender can enter the area, which may involve the emptying of the opposite channel.

2. Remove channels and look for outcomes when defending in wide areas.

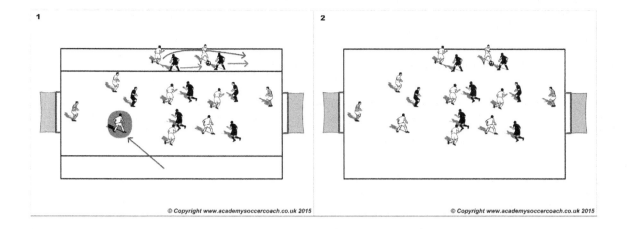

CHALLENGES / QUESTIONS FOR PLAYERS:

- Can you defend 1 v 1 or 2 v 2 in wide areas?

- If you cannot regain possession 1 v 1, can you stop crosses being played?

- Can you deal with moments when you have to defend 1 v 2 as per the Defending when Outnumbered Principles of Play?

- When defending an attack on the opposite side, can you leave the channel, 'tuck in' and become compact with the other defenders?

- When 2 v 2, can defenders make a decision about who tracks the runner and who stays with the player with the ball?

- If a cross does come in, are the defenders in a position to protect the goal? Can the supporting midfielders drop into positions to gather in knockdowns, etc?

- Can the goalkeeper help by coming to catch, punch or just communicate with defenders?

- Can you counter-attack quickly upon regaining possession?

SCORING:

Goals scored. Double the goals scored as a result of an attack from wide areas if necessary.

CAUTION:

There is no need to condition the game so that players 'must' score from crosses. In all games players should have the opportunity to attack the goal in the best, most appropriate way possible. With the parameters in place, this should happen naturally. Give teams double-points for a goal resulting from a wide attack (as above) to offer an incentive.

38: Defending Crosses Phase of Play

PURPOSE OF SESSION:

Players practice defending crosses and attacks from wide areas.

INITIAL SET-UP:

- Whites v. Blacks play in the playing area.

- Blacks have two wide players stationed in each orange channel.

- A goalkeeper defends a big goal with the White defenders and the Blacks defend three smaller goals.

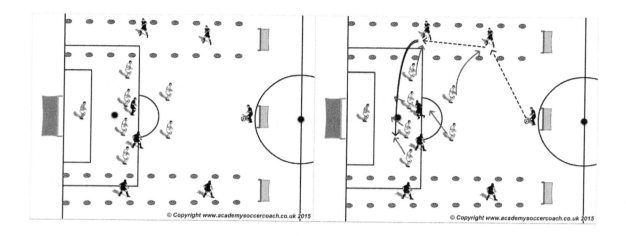

© Copyright www.academysoccercoach.co.uk 2015   © Copyright www.academysoccercoach.co.uk 2015

INSTRUCTIONS:

- The White defending team are set up with a goalkeeper, four defenders and two central midfielders.

- The White defenders are allowed into the wide zones, but the Black wide players are confined to the outer channels.

- Blacks attack the goal in any way they wish, though they are encouraged to attack through the wide players.

- **TRANSITION:** Once the defending team regains possession, they can attack and score in any of the three smaller goals.

PROGRESSIONS:

1. Add extra players to the Black attacking team to increase the 'stress' on the defending team.

2. Opposite Black wide attackers can now join in the attack to further increase the pressure on the defenders.

CHALLENGES / QUESTIONS FOR PLAYERS:

- Can a combination of full-back and defensive midfielder confine wide players to the wide channels and not allow any crosses?

- Can the rest of the back four become 'compact' and position themselves across the width of the goal to defend crosses?

- Can midfielder players pick up any loose balls that drop following a cross?

- Can the goalkeeper come and catch / punch crosses when appropriate?

- When the ball is in and around the box, can you defend *critically* to prevent a goal?

- Can you counter-attack quickly and with some composure to score in any of the three goals?

- When you become disorganized, can you reorganize quickly and compactly?

SCORING:

Attackers score in the big goal, the defending team score in any three of the smaller goals.

CAUTION:

It is often harder to score in one big goal than to counter-attack into three smaller ones. Give attackers extra points for a goal to even up the contest.

39: Stay On Your Feet SSG

PURPOSE OF SESSION:

To get players into the habit of staying on their feet while defending, and choosing wisely when to go to ground.

INITIAL SET-UP:

- Whites v. Blacks play in the playing area.

- Two goalkeepers defend two goals.

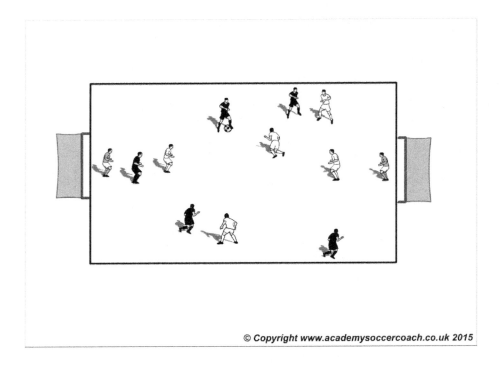

© Copyright www.academysoccercoach.co.uk 2015

INSTRUCTIONS:

- The Black attacking team is permitted two-touches only. This will help their first touch and awareness, but will also encourage the defending team to stay on their feet, rather than to dive into tackles.

- **TRANSITION:** Natural transitions occur in small-sided games.

PROGRESSIONS:

1. It is important that the coach is age and ability conscious. Increase the touch limit if players are young to allow the game to flow more.

2. Allow all players to play off as many touches as required – is there evidence that they stay on their feet more?

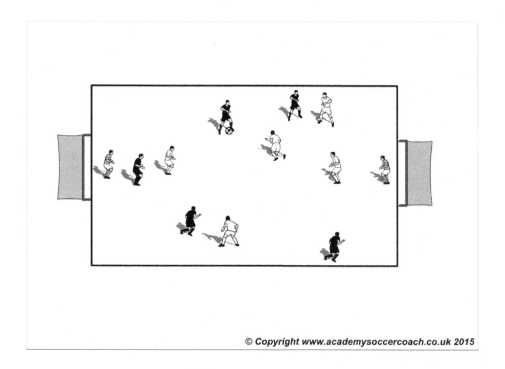

CHALLENGES / QUESTIONS FOR PLAYERS:

- Can you pressure the opponent enough to spoil the chance of him playing off only two touches?

- Can you stay on your feet, forcing the opponent to play a rushed pass?

- Can you force the opponent to play backwards or give the ball away?

- Once the game is free, can you decide effectively when you need to go to ground?

- Can you defend *critically* when the situation arises?

- Once possession is regained, can you counter-attack effectively?

SCORING:

Goals scored.

CAUTION:

Change restrictions if players cannot cope with playing off two-touches only.

40: Tracking Forward Runs

PURPOSE OF SESSION:

To encourage players to recognize and track forward runs made by their immediate opponent.

INITIAL SET-UP:

- Whites v. Blacks play in the playing area.
- An end zone (for scoring) is placed at either end of the pitch.

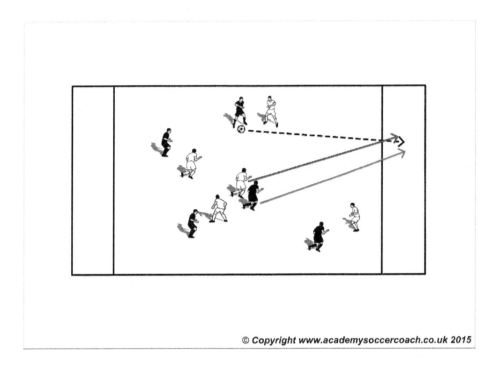

INSTRUCTIONS:

- Players play 5v5 / 6v6 etc. in the playing area. A goal is scored by passing to a forward runner who stops the ball in the end zone.
- Players should 'man-mark' a particular opponent.
- Players should not enter the end zone before the ball does.
- **TRANSITION:** Natural transitions occur in small-sided games.

PROGRESSIONS:

1. Add 'bounce' players on the outside who have one touch to play passes either back to a teammate or who provide an assist by passing into the end zone. Other players, who sense a dangerous forward run, can now move to cover this run.
2. Add goals and goalkeepers and monitor whether players are tracking more forward runs.

CHALLENGES / QUESTIONS FOR PLAYERS:

- Can you open your body and recognize the intentions of your immediate opponent?

- Can you mentally track his movements?

- Can you physically track his forward runs to prevent him from scoring?

- When should you mark touch tight, and when should you allow space between you and your opponent?

- As a covering defender, can you leave your immediate opponent if you sense danger from a different forward runner?

- Can you transition quickly and counter-attack while opponents are disorganized?

SCORING:

Goals scored.

CAUTION:

Change players around the outside when appropriate.

41: Tracking Runs from Midfield

PURPOSE OF SESSION:

To allow players to practice tracking forward runs from midfield areas.

INITIAL SET-UP:

- Whites v. Blacks play in a playing area that is divided into thirds.

- One attacker and one defender are locked in the end zones. Teams play 3 v 3 or 4 v 4 in the larger central zone.

- Each team attacks and defends two small goals.

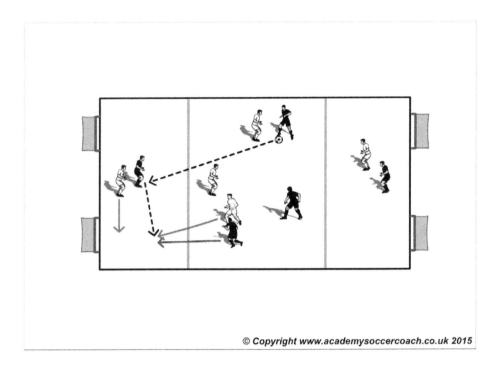

INSTRUCTIONS:

- Central players can either score directly into one of the small goals or pass into the attacking player in the end zone.

- To score, the striker can either turn to shoot, or lay the ball off for an attacking run from midfield. A defending midfield player should track this forward run.

- **TRANSITION:** Natural transitions occur as the ball changes hands.

PROGRESSIONS:

1. Two midfield players can now join in attacks (and both will therefore need tracking).
2. Add big goals and goalkeepers.

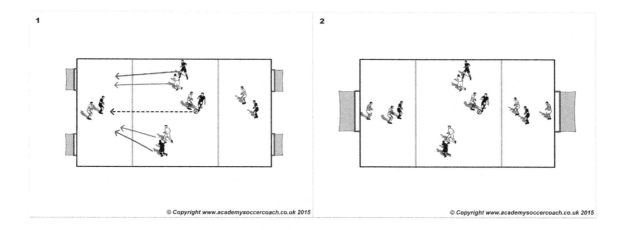

CHALLENGES / QUESTIONS FOR PLAYERS:

- Can you open your body and recognize the intentions of your immediate opponent?

- Can you mentally track his movements?

- Can you physically track his forward runs to prevent him from scoring?

- When should you mark touch tight, and when should you allow space between you and your opponent?

- As a covering defender, can you leave your immediate opponent if you sense danger from a different forward runner?

- Can the midfielders, with the help of their covering center-back, stop opponents scoring directly from the central zone?

- Can the center-back spoil the first touch of the striker?

- Can you transition quickly and counter-attack while opponent players are disorganized?

SCORING:

Goals scored.

CAUTION:

Make a call as to whether you allow midfield players to score directly into the goals. Depending on the group it may be too easy or too hard. By allowing direct goals, it allows the center-back greater returns. (Do I cover the goal as a priority? Do I mark tightly? Etc.)

42: Outnumbered SSG

PURPOSE OF SESSION:

A session for intentionally creating outnumbered situations for a team to defend.

INITIAL SET-UP:

- Whites v. Blacks play in the playing area.

- One goal is defended by a goalkeeper. There is one server opposite, playing for the White team.

- Two scoring areas are set up several yards from the end line as shown.

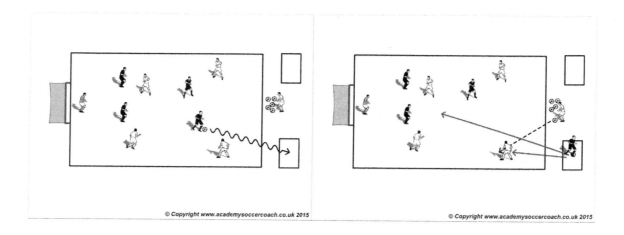

INSTRUCTIONS:

- White server starts by passing a ball into the White team which attempt to score in the big goal.

- The Black team look to defend this and counter-attack by dribbling the ball into a scoring area. The Black player will be unopposed as soon as he leaves the playing area.

- Once the Black scorer is out of the game, the server restarts the game immediately and the Blacks are outnumbered.

- The out of position Black player must recover quickly.

- **TRANSITION:** This exercise is an adaptation of a small-sided game so natural transitions occur as the ball changes hands.

PROGRESSIONS:

1. The White server can join the attacks to further outnumber the opposition.

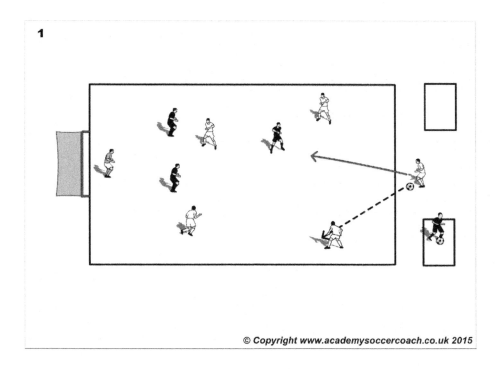

CHALLENGES / QUESTIONS FOR PLAYERS:

- Can the outnumbered team *delay* the attack to allow their teammate to recover?
- Can they *deny* the opposition forward passes?
- Can they *deflect* opponents away from goal?
- Can they *defend critically* when required?
- Can the Black scorer recover quickly?
- Does the Black scorer recover to the ball and try to tackle? Or does he recover to a position between the ball and the goal?
- Can the team counter-attack wisely and be immediately ready to defend when outnumbered?

SCORING:

Count the number of White goals versus the number of Black dribbles into the scoring areas.

CAUTION:

Being outnumbered becomes more pronounced with fewer players on the pitch.

43: Defending Against Direct Play SSG

PURPOSE OF SESSION:

For players to practice defending against long, direct passes towards the goal area.

INITIAL SET-UP:

- Whites v. Blacks play in the playing area.

- Two players from each team are placed outside the pitch.

- Two goals and two goalkeepers, as per normal.

© Copyright www.academysoccercoach.co.uk 2015

INSTRUCTIONS:

- Both teams play a small-sided game and look to score as normal.

- When one of the outside players receives the ball, he must play a long direct pass towards the opponent's goal area.

- The opposition defend accordingly.

- **TRANSITION:** Natural transitions occur in small-sided games.

PROGRESSIONS:

1. The outside players now play inside, as per normal. Observe how defenders deal with direct play.

© Copyright www.academysoccercoach.co.uk 2015

CHALLENGES / QUESTIONS FOR PLAYERS:

- Can you pick up the visual cues of when a player is going to try a long, direct pass?

- When a teammate is going to head / control the ball, can the other defenders narrow off and cover behind him?

- Can you quickly 'squeeze' out of the scoring zone once the danger has passed?

- Can you recover quickly into shape when possession is lost?

- Can you stop strikers turning, or spoil the pass into their feet?

- Can you defend *critically* to see off any danger?

- Can you win headers, make blocks, and compete for knockdowns?

- Can you counter-attack effectively and reorganize once disorganized?

SCORING:

Goals scored.

CAUTION:

Maintain a balance between encouraging long passes for the purposes of defending outcomes (i.e. to defend against direct play), and emphasizing that this direct style may be in contrast to your normal attacking strategy.

44: Defending In & Around the Box

PURPOSE OF SESSION:

To create chaos, close to goal, to allow players to practice defending *critically* in and around the penalty area.

INITIAL SET-UP:

- Whites v. Blacks play in the penalty area.
- Two goals with two goalkeepers.

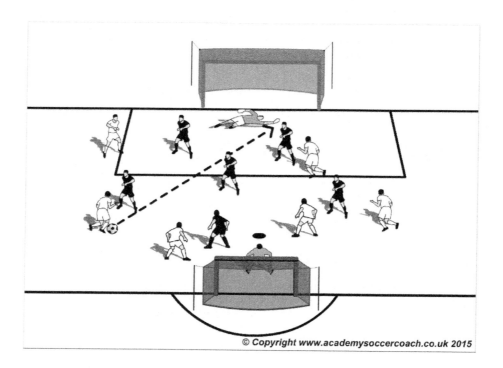

© Copyright www.academysoccercoach.co.uk 2015

INSTRUCTIONS:

- Players play 5v5 / 6v6 etc. in the penalty area.
- As the game is within the penalty area, insist that players "shoot on sight" to keep defenders on their toes.
- **TRANSITION:** Natural transitions occur in small-sided games.

PROGRESSIONS:

1. Outnumber one team to further handicap them and make defending even more *critical*.

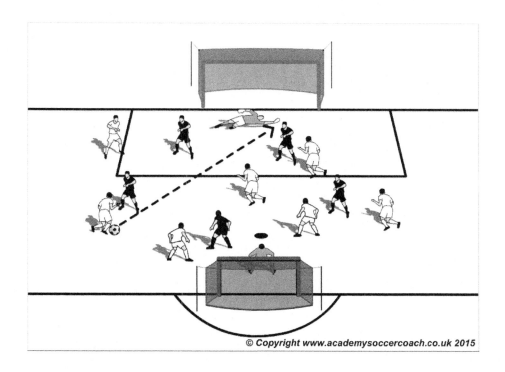

CHALLENGES / QUESTIONS FOR PLAYERS:

- Can you press the player with the ball and stop him shooting / scoring (insist that players press the ball as virtually every situation requires them to defend *critically*)?

- A player should not get more than two touches in the penalty area.

- Can you show players away from goal?

- Can you force them to try to pass, rather than shoot?

- If one player presses the ball, ensure the rest of the team are prepared to press after him.

- Once you intercept, can you attempt to counter-attack and score quickly?

SCORING:

Goals scored.

CAUTION:

Ensure players' safety against a player who shoots hard – there is not much room to get out of the way! I have played this game with 18 players – any more and I have created a third team who play as 'bounce' players along the outside.

Scenarios

45: Keep a Clean Sheet

PURPOSE:

For players to prioritize keeping a clean sheet.

SCENARIO:

Players are challenged to keep a clean sheet for 10 minutes, which will see them into the next round of a knock-out competition. They are also slightly outnumbered. As an incentive, 30 seconds is knocked off the clock each time they are able to pass to their lone striker in the end zone (this is to prevent the players just kicking the ball away aimlessly or out of play).

INITIAL SET-UP:

- Blacks v. Whites in the area shown.

- Whites defend one big goal with a goalkeeper and attack by passing into their striker in the end zone.

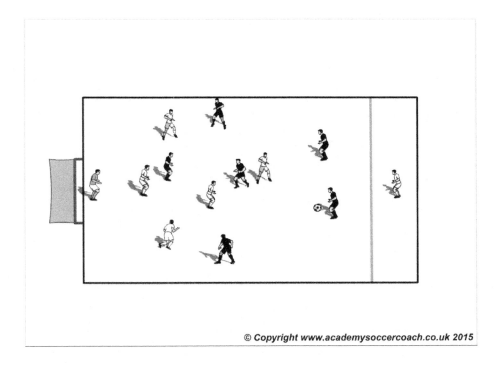

INSTRUCTIONS:

- White defending team has one less outfield player.

- Challenge them to use the Defending Principles of Play to keep a clean sheet.

- The Black team is challenged to go on an all-out attack.

- **TRANSITION:** Whites focus their transitions on getting the ball to their striker.

PROGRESSIONS:

1. Switch strategy so that Black team is now challenged to keep a clean sheet.

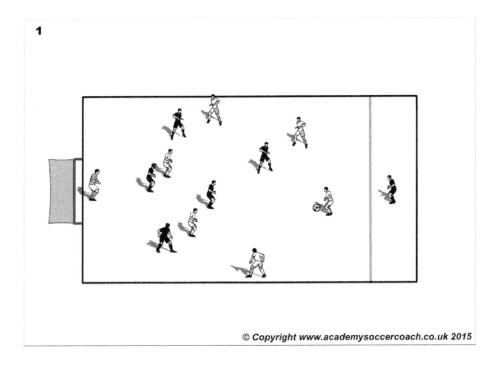

© Copyright www.academysoccercoach.co.uk 2015

CHALLENGES / QUESTIONS FOR PLAYERS:

- Can the players come up with a strategy to keep a clean sheet?

- Can they defend compactly and within the Defending Principles of Play?

- Can they defend *critically*, with composure when required?

- Can they mentally handle the pressure without panicking, staying focused and by making clear decisions?

- Can they formulate ways of counter-attacking to help them run the clock down?

SCORING:

The defending team wins if they keep a clean sheet for 10 minutes They can reduce the time on the clock by successfully passing to their striker. The attacking team looks to score a winning goal.

If running the clock down does not suit your group, challenge them to see which team can keep a clean sheet for longest! By transitioning and passing the ball into their striker, they get a 30-second bonus.

CAUTION:

Watch out for occasions when a team concedes quickly and becomes deflated. Try asking them to analyze their strategy and encourage them to try again – even if it is just for five minutes!

46: Defending a Lead

PURPOSE:

For players to practice defending with a narrow lead.

SCENARIO:

Your team is winning 1-0 going into the last 10 minutes of a cup final. They must hang on to win, or add a second goal via a counter-attack.

INITIAL SET-UP:

- Can be played 11v11 or any game format that suits (e.g. 4v4, 5v5, 8v8 etc.).

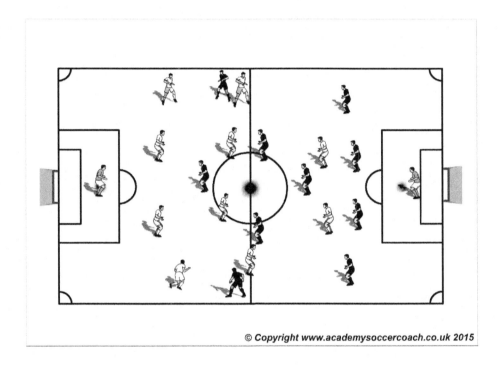

© Copyright www.academysoccercoach.co.uk 2015

INSTRUCTIONS:

- Play a 10-minute game – both teams have even numbers.
- Whites attack as required to score an equalizing goal.
- Ask the Black team to be disciplined and devise a game plan.
- **TRANSITION:** Natural transitions occur in small-sided games.

PROGRESSIONS:

1. Example of 5 v 5 game.
2. Example of 8 v 8 game.

3. Change formation / strategy during session to meet particular needs.

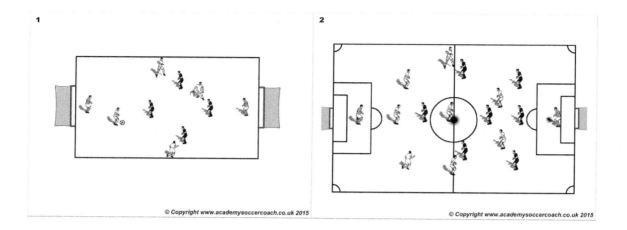

© Copyright www.academysoccercoach.co.uk 2015   © Copyright www.academysoccercoach.co.uk 2015

CHALLENGES / QUESTIONS FOR PLAYERS:

- Can every individual player contribute to the defending strategy?

- Can the team remain 'compact' when out of possession?

- Can we press / drop and offer cover, balance and support when defending when organized?

- Can we delay, deny, deflect attacks when the team becomes disorganized?

- Can you mentally deal with heavy pressure from the opposition?

- Can you defend *critically* when required?

- Can you counter-attack when the opportunity presents itself?

- If you do counter-attack, what players should join in, and which players should remain defensively disciplined?

- If we see very little of the ball, can we retain it when we do win possession?

SCORING:

Normal goals apply.

CAUTION:

Watch out for players either forgetting or neglecting the scenario as it is "just training". Ensure they engage with the aims and objectives of the exercise.

47: Defending an Away Goal

PURPOSE:

For players to practice defending with an 'away' goal.

SCENARIO:

It is the second leg of a two-legged tie. It is 1-1 from your away leg and it is 0-0 entering the last 15 minutes of your home game. If your team holds out, and does not concede, they go through to the next round. However, if they concede, they will go out. Can your team balance defence and attack?

INITIAL SET-UP:

- Can be played 11v11 or any game format that suits (e.g. 4v4, 5v5, 8v8 etc).

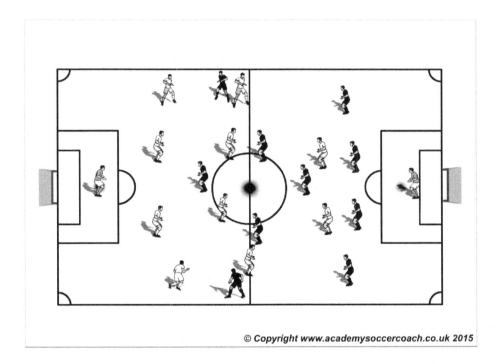

INSTRUCTIONS:

- Play a 15-minute game – both teams have even numbers.

- Whites attack as required to score a winning goal.

- Ask Black team to be disciplined and devise a game plan to cater for (a) seeing the game out at 0-0, (b) scoring a goal to win, and (c) reacting to going 1-0 down.

- **TRANSITION:** Natural transitions occur in small-sided games.

PROGRESSIONS:

1. Example of 5 v 5 game.

2. Example of 8 v 8 game.

3. Change formation / strategy should either team score, thus adapting to the changed scenario.

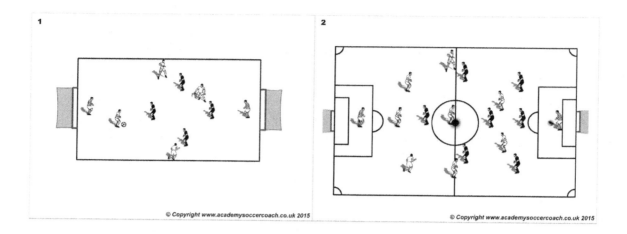

© Copyright www.academysoccercoach.co.uk 2015   © Copyright www.academysoccercoach.co.uk 2015

CHALLENGES / QUESTIONS FOR PLAYERS:

- Can all players contribute to the defending strategy?

- Can the team become organized and 'compact' without the ball?

- Can the players defend according the Defending Principles of Play?

- Can we delay, deny, deflect attacks when the team becomes disorganized?

- Can you mentally deal with heavy pressure from the opposition as they press to score a goal?

- Can you defend *critically* when required?

- Can you counter-attack when the opportunity arises? Which players join in, and which players remain defensively disciplined, when counter-attacking?

- If we see very little of the ball, can we make good use of it when we win possession?

- Can you adapt to changing circumstances should either team score?

SCORING:

Normal goals apply.

CAUTION:

Again, ensure players engage with the scenario.

48: Defending Under Constant Pressure

PURPOSE:

For players to practice defending when under heavy pressure from the opposition.

SCENARIO:

Your team is 1-0 up with ten minutes of a game remaining. The aim is for the winning team to hold onto their lead. However, the referee (you, the coach) constantly gives free-kicks and corners to the opposition (never 'punish' a player by awarding an unjust free-kick when he has defended well). If the ball goes out of play, the opposition will always restart in possession.

INITIAL SET-UP:

- Can be played 11v11 or any game format that suits (e.g. 4v4, 5v5, 8v8 etc).

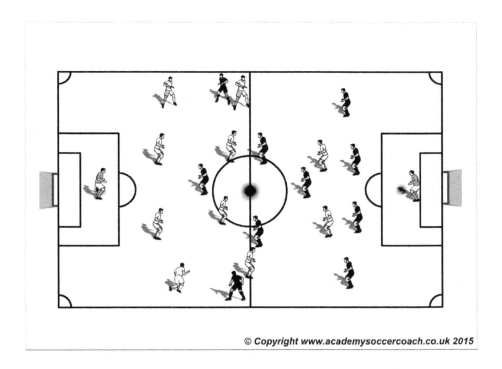

© Copyright www.academysoccercoach.co.uk 2015

INSTRUCTIONS:

- Play a 10-minute game – both teams have even numbers.

- Whites attack as required to score a winning goal.

- Ask Black team to be disciplined; they will be heavily challenged to defend *critically*.

- **TRANSITION:** Natural transitions occur in small-sided games.

PROGRESSIONS:

1. Example of 5 v 5 game.

2. Example of 8 v 8 game.

3. Change formation / strategy as necessary.

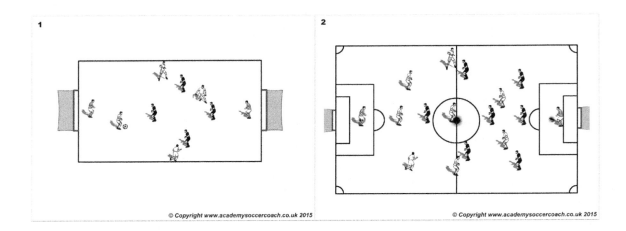

CHALLENGES / QUESTIONS FOR PLAYERS:

*   Can all players follow the game strategy for the scenario to be successful?

*   Can the team remain 'compact' when out of possession?

*   When organized, can the players press / drop and offer cover, balance and support?

*   When disorganized, can the players play within the Principles of Defending when outnumbered?

*   Can you mentally deal with increasing pressure from the opposition?

*   Can you mentally deal with unjust decisions from the referee and remain focused?

*   Can the team defend critically when they are required to?

*   Can you counter-attack when the opportunity arises?

*   Players should decide how many players (and which players specifically) they want to commit to a counter-attack?

*   If we see very little of the ball, can we retain it when we do win possession? Remember that if the ball goes out of play at all, the opposition will restart the game with possession again.

SCORING:

Normal goals apply.

CAUTION:

Do not allow players to get cranky because the rules are deemed "unfair". Challenge them to rise to the problems set before them.

49: Two Up – Two Down

PURPOSE:

For players to switch their mentality from all-out attacking to all-out defending.

SCENARIO:

There are two 10-minute halves. One team plays the first 10 minutes with two extra players. Goals scored by the team with numerical superiority count double, meaning they must attack and score as many goals as possible. During the second 10-minute period, the opposition has two extra players. Can the outnumbered team defend strongly against numerically superior teams looking to attack, score lots of goals and adjust the score line?

INITIAL SET-UP:

- Can be played with numbers 7 v 5 and above.

- Two goals defended by two goalkeepers.

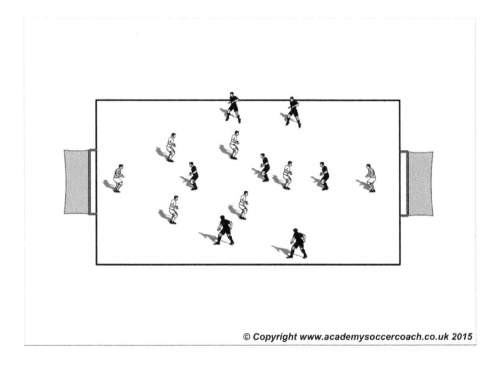

INSTRUCTIONS:

- Play two 10-minute games – the Black team has two extra players to start with.

- Blacks attack relentlessly for first half in search of as many goals as possible.

- **TRANSITION:** Natural transitions occur in small-sided games.

PROGRESSIONS:

1. Team which were previously outnumbered (Whites) have two extra players for the second half.

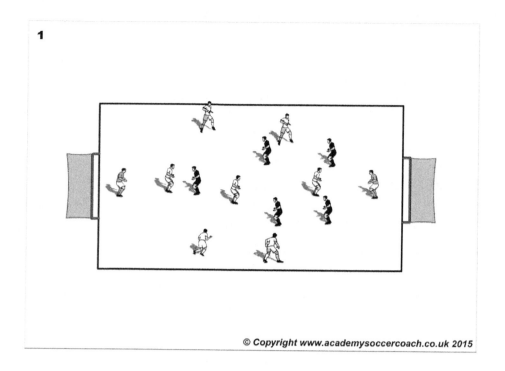

CHALLENGES / QUESTIONS FOR PLAYERS:

- When the opposition's goals are worth double, can you defend resolutely for the duration?
- If you have a lead, can you hold on to it with two fewer players?
- Can you apply the Principles of Defending when Outnumbered?
- Can you *delay* attacks or *deny* opponent's forward passes?
- Can you *deflect* or force them away from goal?
- Can you defend *critically* in and around the goal?
- Can you reorganize quickly should you become disorganized?
- Even when two players down, can you counter-attack sensibly and get a goal?

SCORING:

Normal goals apply. Goals from the team with numerical superiority count as double.

CAUTION:

You may find that the outnumbered team are actually winning – to the frustration of their opponents! Choose your teams wisely to help facilitate the scenario.

50: Defending with 10 Men

PURPOSE:

For older players – playing 11 v 11 soccer – to practice defending with one less man.

SCENARIO:

Your team has been reduced to ten men following an injury or sending off. There are 15 minutes to go – can you defend strongly and hold out? The team may be leading 1-0 and holding on for the win, or it may be 0-0 and they are holding out for a draw.

INITIAL SET-UP:

- Full pitch as per a 'real' game. Normal rules of soccer apply.
- 10 Black players (focus) versus 11 White players.

© Copyright www.academysoccercoach.co.uk 2015

INSTRUCTIONS:

- Play a 15-minute match – 11 Whites versus 10 Blacks.
- Whites attack as required to break down the 10-man Black team.
- Ask Black team to be disciplined and devise a game plan.
- **TRANSITION:** Natural transitions occur as in a normal soccer game.

PROGRESSIONS:

1. Team plays 1-4-3-1 (depending on team beliefs, philosophy and strategy).

2. Team plays 1-5-3-1 (depending on team beliefs, philosophy and strategy).

3. Change formation / strategy during session to meet particular needs.

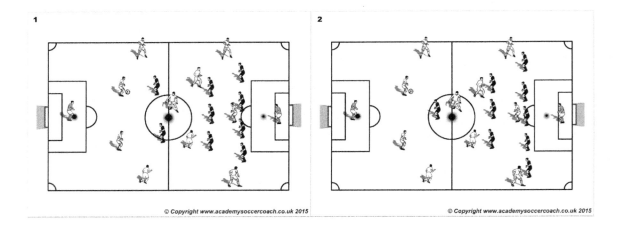

CHALLENGES / QUESTIONS FOR PLAYERS:

- Can all players contribute to the defending strategy?

- Can the team become compact and difficult to penetrate when out of possession?

- Can we *delay, deny, deflect* attacks when disorganized?

- Can you remain mentally strong when asked to defend for long, sustained periods?

- Can you defend *critically* when the goal is under threat?

- Can you counter-attack sensibly when appropriate?

- Can we make good use of any ball possession we get (retain the ball, counter-attack)?

SCORING:

Normal goals apply.

CAUTION:

As players get older, the chances of having to play 10 v 11 increases. It is rarely something a team will practice specifically for, in the build up to a game, so it is important that the players understand the Principles of Defending When Outnumbered, and will have some experience of a strategy when playing with one less player.

Other Books in this Series:

- **Deliberate Soccer Practice:** 50 Passing & Possession Football Exercises to Improve Decision-Making

- **Deliberate Soccer Practice:** 50 Small-Sided Football Exercises to Improve Decision-Making

- **Deliberate Soccer Practice:** 50 Attacking Football Exercises to Improve Decision-Making

Other Books by Ray Power:

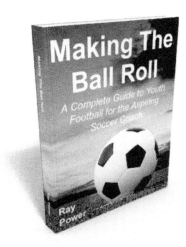

Making The Ball Roll: A Complete Guide to Youth Football for the Aspiring Soccer Coach by Ray Power

Making the Ball Roll is the ultimate complete guide to coaching youth soccer.

This focused and easy-to-understand book details training practices and tactics, and goes on to show you how to help young players achieve peak performance through tactical preparation, communication, psychology, and age-specific considerations. Each chapter covers, in detail, a separate aspect of coaching to give you, the football coach, a broad understanding of youth soccer development. Each topic is brought to life by the stories of real coaches working with real players. Never before has such a comprehensive guide to coaching soccer been found in the one place. If you are a new coach, or just trying to improve your work with players - and looking to invest in your future - this is a must-read book!

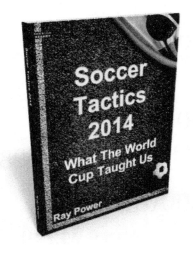

Soccer Tactics 2014: What The World Cup Taught Us by Ray Power

World Cups throw up unique tactical variations. Countries and football cultures from around the globe converge, in one place, to battle it out for world soccer supremacy. The 2014 World Cup in Brazil was no different, arguably throwing up tactical differences like never seen at a competition in modern times. Contests are not just won by strong work ethics and technical brilliance, but by tactical discipline, fluidity, effective strategies, and (even) unique national traits.

Soccer Tactics 2014 analyses the intricacies of modern international systems, through the lens of matches in Brazil. Covering formations, game plans, key playing positions, and individuals who bring football tactics to life - the book offers analysis and insights for soccer coaches, football players, and fans the world over. The book sheds light on where football tactics currently stand... and where they are going. Includes analysis of group matches, knock out stages, and the final.

CPSIA information can be obtained at www.ICGtesting.com
Printed in the USA
BVOW09s1240121016

464820BV00005B/38/P